D1613905

TIFFANY PEARLS

JOHN LORING

ABRAMS, NEW YORK

CONTENTS

A pearl! A perfect world enclosed in her sphere . . . iridescing with light more lunar than solar.

—RENÉ HUYGHE, 1979 (curator of the Musée du Louvre, member of the Académie Française)

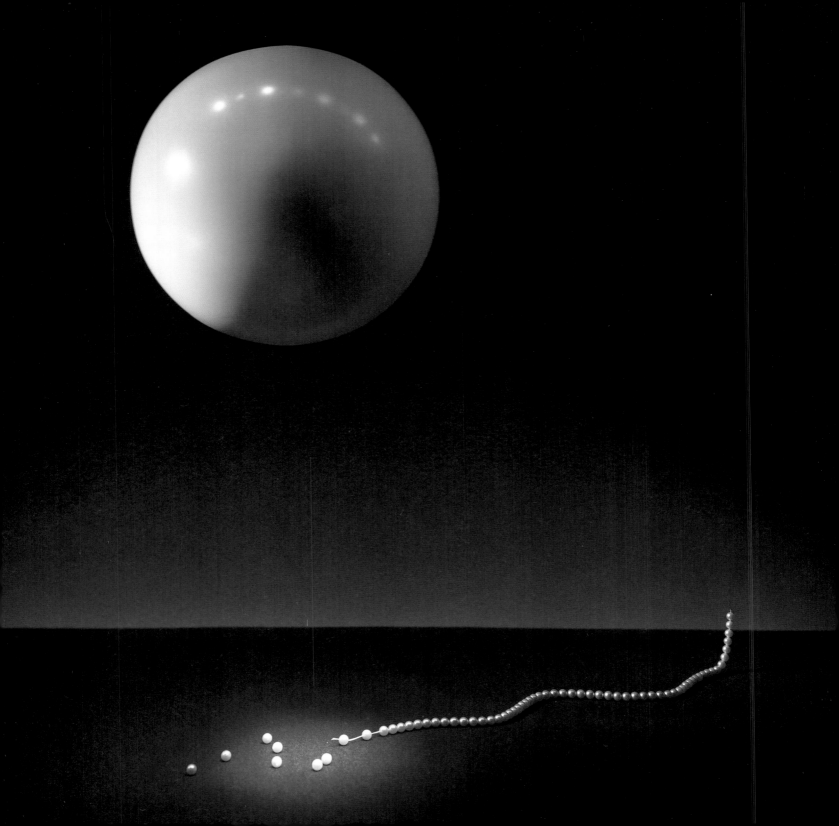

INTRODUCTION   "Pearls of wisdom." "A pearl among women." "A pearl of great worth." These traditional accolades belong to pearls, the only gem perfect in itself, its natural beauty unaided by cutting, faceting, or polishing. • The ancients esteemed these marvels above gemstones, ranking them *Prima Candidarum Gemmarum* (if we are to believe the historian Isidore of Seville); and over two thousand years ago, they were so loved by Egypt's romantic queen Cleopatra and her paramour Julius Caesar that Caesar went so far as to invade Britain in 55 BC in search of pearls (which were once abundant in Scotland's rivers). • In Ravenna, pearls of imperial proportions are immortalized in the famous sixth-century Byzantine mosaics of the emperor Justinian and the empress Theodora. Pearls were the favorite adornment of the prodigiously rich Mogul shahs and, later, Indian potentates. Once discovered as being in profusion in the Americas in the early 1500s, pearls were imported to Europe, where they were the preferred symbol of wealth, rank, and authority among Europe's rulers. The most famous of those, Queen Elizabeth I of England, was not only draped in pearl necklaces, but she had so many pearls stitched to her dresses that she was literally upholstered in pearls, as were—to only a slightly lesser extent—the ladies of the reigning Valois family of France and the Habsburgs of Spain and Austria.

Little has changed today, as pearls enjoy an unbounded popularity, which began in earnest the moment affordable cultured pearls (with Tiffany's blessing) took the lead less than fifty years ago, superseding in many cases the rare and extravagantly priced fine natural pearls of the Persian Gulf, Ceylon, and the South Seas.

Is it true that Cleopatra dissolved a priceless pearl in a glass of wine to impress Mark Antony with the fabled wealth of Egypt? The ever-popular myth has glamour and panache; however, pearls don't give up their luster for a glass of wine, even in the hands of Egypt's seductive queen. And is it true that two thousand years later, New York socialite Mrs. Morton F. "Maisie" Plant traded a two-strand necklace of fifty-five pearls for her magnificent five-story cut-stone mansion on the southeast corner of Fifth Avenue and Fifty-second Street? So goes New York folklore. Her family said she did. Her stepdaughter remembers her explaining in later life (she was thirty-three when the Plant mansion changed hands in 1916), "It wasn't a wise investment, but my husband had lots of money—it didn't matter to him at all." But the *New York Times* in reporting the sale on October 4, 1916 disagreed, saying that William K. Vanderbilt bought the Plant mansion for $1 million. Perhaps he threw in a pearl necklace to sweeten the deal.

Confusing the legend but revealing much about pearls, on December 4, 1962, the *New York Times* revised its story: "The Plants reportedly exchanged the building for a necklace of 55 oriental pearls valued at $1,500,000 . . . Sold at auction in January 1957, the pearls brought $151,000."

Why such a low auction price for the legendary Plant necklace? The price for the natural-pearl ornament simply reflected the phenomenal popularity of cultured pearls, then readily available in the world of fine jewelry thanks largely to Tiffany & Co., which played a leading role by introducing important collections of fine cultured South Sea pearls to the public. At the landmark Fifth Avenue store, Tiffany's gave its all-important official stamp of approval to these beautiful newcomers to its kingdom of precious gems. The result of all this was a vertiginous drop in the price of natural pearls.

In 1902 Florida East Coast Railroad czar Henry Morrison Flagler is believed, according to popular legend, to have paid Tiffany & Co. $2 million for a sixty-inch strand of pearls for his young wife, Mary Lily.

In the 1920s a thirty-inch opera-length strand of flawless natural oriental pearls from Tiffany & Co. could cost over $1 million. Naturally, such

LEFT
Mary, Queen of Scots, wearing the pearls later known as the Hanoverian Pearls (see pages 31, 35, 37, and 41), which she received from Catherine de Médicis as a wedding present in 1558 when she married the dauphin (who acceded as Francis II of France in 1559 and died in 1560). This portrait was copied from a miniature probably painted in France when Mary was in mourning. In November 1894 Tiffany's exhibited another miniature of Mary, Queen of Scots, painted in 1577 when she was Queen Elizabeth's prisoner; that miniature had been loaned to Tiffany's for copying.

OPPOSITE
Queen Elizabeth I circa 1588, portrait attributed to George Gower. The queen's crown, hair, and dress are more than abundantly adorned with pearls. She purchased six of these pearl necklaces in 1568 from her ill-fated cousin, Mary, Queen of Scots. They were later part of the Hanoverian Pearls.

prices limited the market for natural pearls and encouraged the popularity of blatant imitations throughout the '20s, '30s and '40s. Cultured South Sea pearls changed all that in the '50s. Mrs. Plant's double strand of fine oriental pearls was no less beautiful in 1957 than it had been in 1916, but its supposed value had declined by 90 percent, as traditional natural pearls brought relatively the same price in 1957 as their younger cousins, cultured South Sea pearls.

Like the history of all things bright, beautiful, and precious, the history of pearls has its star attractions. Cleopatra's pearl earrings were, of course, the first to achieve world celebrity. Pliny called them "the singular and onely jewels of the world and even nature's wonder." Unfortunately, he neglected to note their shape or size, but he did initiate that myth of one of the earrings' pearls being dissolved in wine to satisfy a wager between the Egyptian queen and Mark Antony. The other pearl, history tells us, was eventually taken to Rome, cut in two, and remade into a pair of earrings for the statue of Venus in the Pantheon.

The much publicized purchase—at auction in New York on January 23, 1969—of "La Peregrina" pearl by Richard Burton as a Valentine's Day

Tiffany & Co. diamond-and-pearl-studded silver frame for a portrait miniature depicting Anne de Pisseleu, Duchess of Étampes (1508–1585), lavishly arrayed in pearls. She was a mistress of Francis I, who undoubtedly obtained the pearls from Spain. Called "the most beautiful of intellectuals and the most intellectual of beauties," the duchess sponsored the Protestant cause, arousing strong opposition. Tiffany's made the frame for its 1885 exhibition of portrait miniatures.

OPPOSITE LEFT
Elizabeth of Valois (1545–1568), daughter of Henry II and Catherine de Médicis and third wife of Philip II of Spain, wearing exceptionally fine pearls in Alonzo Sanchez Coello's circa 1560 portrait. Her large pearl drop could be the "Peregrina." (see pages 14, 21, 24, 29, and 31).

OPPOSITE RIGHT
Infanta Isabel Clara Eugenia of Spain (1566–1633)—daughter of Philip II and Elizabeth of Valois—as painted by Frans Pourbus the Younger around the time of her marriage (April 10, 1599) to Archduke Albert of Austria. She wears a long necklace of large pearls and a pearl-studded headdress. Isabel Clara Eugenia and her husband were joint rulers of the semiautonomous Spanish Netherlands for more than thirty years; their court in Brussels was considered one of the most brilliant in Europe.

RIGHT
Catherine de Médicis (1519–1589) in a miniature by François Clouet painted about 1555. Catherine was a niece of Pope Clement VII, who gave her a fine set of pearls on the occasion of her 1533 marriage to the Duke of Orléans, who acceded as King Henry II of France in 1547. Catherine gave the pearls to Mary, Queen of Scots, on Mary's 1558 marriage to Catherine's eldest son, who acceded as Francis II in 1559 but died in 1560.

OPPOSITE
Tiffany & Co. diamond-and-pearl
frame for an enameled portrait
brooch depicting Anne of Cleves
(1515–1557), fourth wife of Henry
VIII of England, wearing pearl
necklaces and hair ornaments;
the likeness is based on Hans
Holbein the Younger's portrait
painted at the time of Anne's 1540
marriage. Tiffany's made the
frame for its 1885 exhibition of
portrait miniatures.

RIGHT
Renaissance-revival necklace
of round and baroque pearls,
rubies, sapphires, emeralds,
beryls, and diamonds designed
by Paulding Farnham, circa 1901.
The detachable pendant at back
includes a pearl in a diamond-
studded gold cage. The necklace
is part of a parure that includes
a matching bracelet, brooch,
and earrings.

TIFFANY & CO. EXHIBIT
PARIS EXPOSITION 1900
NECKLACE AND PENDANT
AMERICAN PEARLS, DIAMONDS AND ENAMEL.

present for his wife, Elizabeth Taylor, rekindled the public's fascination
with the famous pearls of the past.

The Peregrina was the most celebrated pearl discovered in American
waters. Found off the coast of either Panama or Venezuela in the mid-1500s
(authorities give "before 1554," 1560, or 1574 as the date of its discovery),
it was taken to Spain by Don Diego de Temes and given to Philip II, king of
Spain (1527–1598), who reputedly gave it to England's queen Mary Tudor
(1516–1558) on their marriage in 1554—an event in London that Philip II
did not attend and an event that the Peregrina (if not discovered until 1560

The wife of Andrei Mateivev, Peter
the Great of Russia's ambassador to
the court of Frederick I of Prussia,
in a circa 1703 portrait painted for
Frederick's wife, Queen Sophie
Charlotte, by Mattäus Des Angles.
She wears an elaborate Russian
pearl headdress and a pearl necklace.
Tiffany gemologist George F. Kunz's
The Book of the Pearl (1908) illustrates
similar Russian noblewomen's pearl
headdresses of the seventeenth
century. The pearls came from
freshwater mussels, *Margaritfera
margaritfera,* found in Russia and its
Baltic provinces.

OPPOSITE

Portrait of Queen Kamamalu of Hawaii
(ca. 1796–1824) in English court
dress. She and her husband, King
Kamehameha II (ca. 1797–1824), went
to England to visit George IV, under
whose protection Kamehameha had
placed his island kingdom. Arriving in
the spring of 1824, the two were
received by foreign secretary Lord
Canning, who commissioned John
Hayter to paint their portraits. The
queen wears a fine double-strand pearl
necklace and pearls in her hair; they
were probably gifts from the British
sovereign. Tragically, both Kamamalu
and Kamehameha died of measles in
London in early July 1824 without
meeting George IV.

or 1574) did not attend either. One story states that it was returned to
Spain by Philip II after Mary's demise in 1558, a most unlikely happening
considering that Philip left England for Spain in 1557. Mary's half-sister
Elizabeth I (1533–1603) would have inherited her sister's jewels—and
with her love of pearls and no great love for her brother-in-law, wouldn't
have been inclined to send anything at all to Spain's unpleasant king.

Even if the Peregrina did travel to London ever so briefly, it later ended
up in the Spanish crown jewels and was happily worn by successive queens
of Spain until Philip V (1683–1746) tried unsuccessfully to sell it. A very
similar pearl was discovered in 1691 and given to Charles II by Don Pedro
de Aponte, Conde del Palmer, who had his new pearl (called *"La Compañera*

ABOVE
Drawing for a varicolored
American freshwater pearl
necklace from the late 1870s.
The design was copied from the
Duchess of Angoulême/Empress
Eugénie necklace shown on
pages 28 and 29.

OPPOSITE
Cultured pearl necklace made
in 2002 from the drawing above.

OPPOSITE

Franz-Xavier Winterhalter's 1853 portrait of Empress Eugénie. She is wearing the Duchess of Angoulême's pearl necklace (shown at right) with the matching earrings that she bought from Storr and Mortimer in London in 1853 for 35,750 francs (about $7,200).

RIGHT

Portrait of the Duchess of Angoulême (1778–1851) by Antoine-Jean Gros. She wears a necklace of nine pear-shaped and thirty-eight round pearls, made by Bapst and given to her circa 1818 by her uncle Louis XVIII. She was the only surviving child of Louis XVI and Marie Antoinette.

de la Peregrina") paired with the Peregrina, and the two mounted as earrings. The Spanish queens wore them until 1734, when they were very possibly destroyed in the fire at the old royal palace in Madrid.

But the possibility remains that the Peregrina escaped. About 1790, Maria Louisa of Parma, wife of Charles IV, had an over–200 grain (50 carat) pearl (the Peregrina weighed 234 grains, and 203.84 grains after being drilled in the nineteenth century) set with a gold and diamond ball cap and a band reassuringly inscribed—and possibly accurate—"*Soy La Peregrina.*"

That pearl's history—Peregrina or no—is clear. In 1808, when Napoléon's army—led by his brother Joseph—conquered Spain and Joseph became its king, the pearl had a new owner who kept it in Spain

until Joseph Bonaparte abdicated in 1813, during the breakup of his brother's empire. Two years later he moved to his house Point Breeze, near Philadelphia in Bordentown, New Jersey, with a number of souvenirs of the First Empire, but the Peregrina was not among them. It would have to wait another 150 years to return to America (where it would grace the neck of Elizabeth Taylor) as Joseph had already given the pearl to Empress Josephine's daughter Hortense de Beauharnais (since 1802 married to his younger brother, Louis Bonaparte, king of Holland). In 1837 it was inherited on Hortense's death by her son Louis Napoléon Bonaparte (later the Emperor Napoléon III), who at the time was in need of money and who was an unlikely heir to the throne of France, then occupied by Louis Philippe. Louis Napoléon sold his famous pearl—but not to the French queen Marie-Amalie, which would have been logical as it had formerly belonged to her aunt, Maria Louisa of Parma. However, Marie-Amalie, mindful of the fate of her other jewel-loving aunt Marie Antoinette, had little fondness for jewels, especially those with royal pedigrees, so Louis Napoléon sold the Peregrina in London to the Marquess of Abercorn (who had it drilled, as it kept falling out of its setting); it remained in his family until it was sold in 1969. Is Elizabeth Taylor's magnificent pearl the original Peregrina? Many believe it is. But in 1969, Victoria Eugenia, ex-queen of Spain insisted that it wasn't.

Unraveling the tangled threads of history in the case of the Peregrina is impossible, but were great pearls not such coveted and enchanting objects, there would be no such surrounding myths.

Of all the great pearls of history, none, however, has had more verifiable adventures and more staying power than the unique collection of pearls known as the Hanoverian pearls. Now among Queen Elizabeth II's collection and in the crown jewels of England, they were originally brought to Rome from the Far East and purchased by Lorenzo II de Medici's brother Pope Clement VII.

In 1533, Clement gave his pearls as a wedding present to his fourteen-year-old niece Catherine de Médicis, wife of Henry II of France. Catherine de Médicis wore her great ropes and drops of pearls on all official occasions, until in 1558 she in turn gave them as a wedding gift to Mary, Queen of Scots, on her marriage to Catherine's eldest son, Francis, who became king of France in 1559. When Francis II died at sixteen, his eighteen-year-old widow, Mary, became the dowager queen; however,

BRIDAL PARURE OF MRS. SENATOR SPRAGUE (*NEE* MISS CHASE), MADE BY TIFFANY & CO.

LEFT

Pearl-and-diamond parure comprising a bracelet, earrings, and a tiara with detachable necklace and brooch, made for Senator William Sprague of Rhode Island to present to his bride, Kate Chase, for their wedding on November 12, 1863, in Washington, D. C. The parure cost Tiffany's $4,319.23; it was sold to Sprague for about $6,000 (see pages 62 and 65). Kate Sprague became Washington's leading hostess, actively promoting the presidential ambitions of her father, Salmon P. Chase (secretary of the treasury and later chief justice of the United States), but Chase's presidential candidacy was outmaneuvered in 1868 and he died in 1871. Kate's marriage underwent strains after her husband lost his fortune in the Panic of 1871, and Kate had a widely known affair with Senator Roscoe Conkling of New York. The Spragues divorced in 1882. Illustration from *Harper's Weekly,* Nov. 23, 1863. *Collection of the New-York Historical Society*

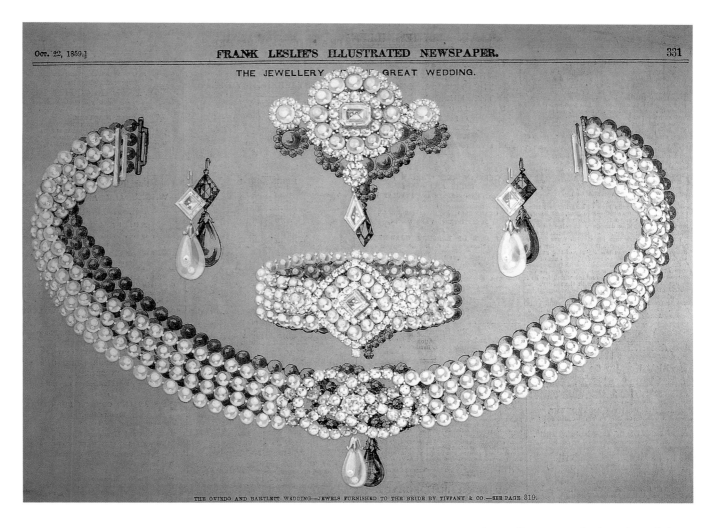

THE JEWELLERY OF THE GREAT WEDDING.

THE OVIEDO AND BARTLETT WEDDING—JEWELS FURNISHED TO THE BRIDE BY TIFFANY & CO.—SEE PAGE 319.

ABOVE

Hand-colored overlay showing the pearl-and-diamond parure made for the wealthy Cuban sugar planter Don Estaban Santa Cruz de Oviedo to present to his bride, Frances Amelia Bartlett, at their wedding on October 13, 1859. The press covered the wedding extensively. The *New-York Times* enthused, "about her neck, itself a pearl, she wore four rows of shapely orient pearl, looped into a festoon by one slight rib of gleaming diamonds, gathered into a knot of love. From this knot depended a single pear-shaped pearl, dipped in diamonds of surpassing lustre and beauty" (Oct. 14, 1859). Others, less effusive, noted that the groom was about six inches shorter and forty years older than the bride. Oviedo died in 1870, and in 1886–1887 the by-then remarried Frances von Glümer sold the parure back to Tiffany's for $9,900, roughly what Oviedo had paid for it. (*Frank Leslie's Illustrated Newspaper,* October 22, 1859)

B
"Queen pearl"
natural size, found in 1857, near Paterson,
New Jersey.

123 grains.

108 grains.

82 grains.

104 grains.

SIZES OF PEARLS.

Catherine de Médicis controlled the country during the minority of her second son, Charles IX, who was then only ten. Catherine had no need of Mary, and in 1561 sent her back to rule Scotland with little else but her clothes and jewels. Her half-brother, Moray, the regent of Scotland, appropriated the greater portion of Mary's jewels and in 1568 sold the six long cordons and about twenty-five very large unstrung pearls from the collection to Queen Elizabeth I for 12,000 crowns.

The queen of Scotland's pearls were considered to be the most magnificent in Europe. They were sent to London and shown to Queen Elizabeth on May 1, 1568.

In a letter to Catherine de Médicis, who wanted the pearls back, the French ambassador to the court of England, Bochetel la Forrest, wrote:

> Queen Elizabeth was complimented with the first offer of them. She saw them yesterday in the presence of the Earls of Pembroke and Leicester, and pronounced them to be of unparalleled beauty. There are six cordons of large pearls, strung as paternosters, but there are five-and-twenty separate from the rest, much finer and larger than those which are strung. These are for the most part like black muscades [a very rare and valuable variety of pearl, having the deep purple color and bloom of the muscatel grape]. They had not been here more than three days, when they were appraised by various merchants, this queen wishing to have them at the sum named by the jeweler, who would have made his profit by selling them again. They were first shown to three or four working jewelers and lapidaries, by whom they were estimated at pound 3,000 sterling [about ten thousand crowns], who offered to give that sum for them. Several Italian merchants came after them, who valued them at twelve thousand crowns, which is the price, as I am told, this queen will take them at. There is a Genevese who saw them after the others, and said they were worth sixteen thousand crowns, but I think they will allow her to have them for twelve thousand. In the meantime I have not delayed giving your Majesty timely notice of what is going on, though I doubt she will allow them to escape her.

The many portraits of Elizabeth I indicate that the pearls were her constant companions. Ironically, they were returned to Mary, Queen of Scots' son James VI of Scotland when he became James I of England in 1603, sixteen

In 1861 President-elect Abraham Lincoln spent $530 at Tiffany's for a seed-pearl parure comprising earrings, a necklace, a brooch, and two bracelets; he gave the parure to his wife, who wore it at the inaugural ball on March 20, 1861. The necklace and bracelets from Mary Todd Lincoln's parure are shown here.

Matthew Brady's inaugural-ball photograph of Mary Todd Lincoln wearing the parure.

years after Queen Elizabeth had had his mother executed for treason. His queen, Anne of Denmark, wore them briefly, then in 1613 the pearls left England, given as a wedding present to James I's daughter Elizabeth when she married Frederick V, Elector Palatine. Little time was wasted before they were again moved, this time to Holland in 1620 after Frederick's defeat at the Battle of White Mountain in the Thirty Years' War.

The pearls' travels continued when one of Elizabeth and Frederick's thirteen children, Sophia, married the Elector of Hanover; their son George eventually became George I of England at the death in 1714 of England's much-loved but heirless Queen Anne. So the fabled pearls of Clement VII; Catherine de Médicis; Mary, Queen of Scots; Elizabeth I; and Elizabeth of Bohemia returned to England.

The Congress of Vienna, which repartitioned Europe in 1815 after Napoléon's defeat at Waterloo, made Hanover a kingdom—so making George IV the king of Hanover as well as the king of England, a distinction shared by his brother and successor, William IV. But when Victoria

Seed-pearl necklace and brooch,
probably made around 1861 for
Tiffany's store at 550 Broadway,
where President-elect Abraham
Lincoln purchased a similar parure
for his wife.

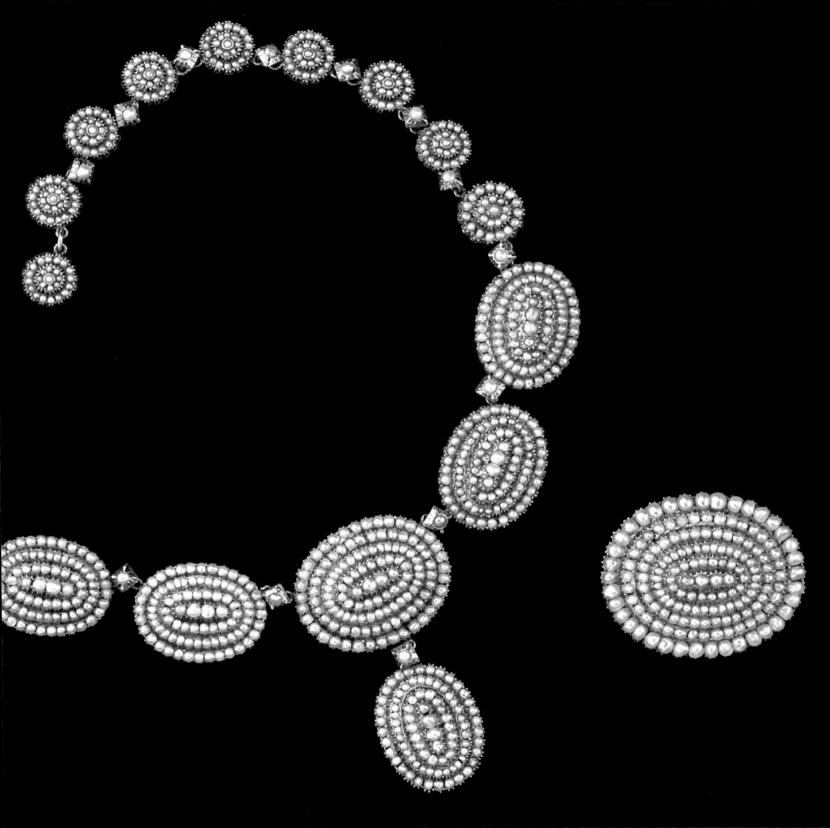

Cameo brooches were the height of fashion in the late 1860s and early 1870s. The best cameos were carved by artisans in Rome or Paris, then mounted by Paris jewelers in gold settings studded with gems. In December 1870 the *Evening Mail* reported that Tiffany's "cameos are much worn and decidedly fashionable. The work is foreign, and when set with diamonds . . . extremely rich. They constitute the favorite presents in the family circle; price of a splendid set, $500." This cameo pendant in a frame decorated with diamonds, fifteen pearls, and five oval pearl drops is marked Tiffany, Reed & Cie., Paris. It was almost certainly designed by Félix Closson and purchased from the jeweler Léon Rouvenat by Gideon F. T. Reed. Closson and Rouvenat's cameo brooches won a gold medal at the 1867 Paris Exposition.

Late 1860s drawings for a pearl-and-diamond brooch and earrings set with the pearl drops that were in vogue in the 1860s and 1870s.

Gold cameo frame with enamel, diamonds, and four pearls, probably also designed by Félix Closson and made by Léon Rouvenat.

became queen of England in 1837, Hanover's Salic Law prevented a woman from inheriting the throne. A new king, Ernest Augustus, was chosen, who demanded the return of the "Hanoverian" pearls. Victoria said "of course"—a vague response—and simply turned the matter of the pearls over to the courts. Twenty-one years later, in 1858 (six years after Ernest Augustus died), Hanover got one splendid necklace of fine pearls (possibly "Hanoverian"), and Victoria kept the rest. And so they remain in England and are worn to this day, reconfigured into modern necklaces, chokers, and earrings.

The sixteenth-century mania for pearls was of course the result of Christopher Columbus's 1498 discovery of the seemingly limitless supply of fine pearls off the coast of Venezuela, concentrated around the islands of Coche, Cubagua, and Margarita. Their discovery merited America the name the "Land of Pearls." It is estimated that between 1513 and 1540 over thirteen tons of Cubagua pearls were taken to Europe by the Spanish.

Drawings for pearl-and-diamond
pendants by the as-yet-unnamed
designer who came to New York
to work at Tiffany & Co. when the
Prussian army besieged Paris in late
1870. He designed a remarkable
body of work in the last quarter
of the nineteenth century. The
drawing opposite features a black
pearl, probably from La Paz in
Baja California. The pearls in both
drawings are beautifully rendered,
and the black pearl's luster and
orient are vividly depicted.

But the Land of Pearls deserved its name for many reasons. From the Gulf
of Mexico to the Gulf of Lower California, from the Mississippi River to
the Ohio River, from Wisconsin, Tennessee, Texas, and Arkansas to New
Jersey, its waters produced an extraordinary variety of fine freshwater and
saltwater pearls.

If Spain had brought to world prominence South America's saltwater
pearls, it was Tiffany & Co. who introduced the world to the beauty and
value of North America's freshwater pearls. In 1857 Tiffany's great adventures with freshwater pearls began.

More pearl-jewelry drawings by
the unnamed designer from Paris.

RIGHT
A pair of diamond earrings
with oval pearl drops—the gray
and white pearls are remarkably
well matched.

OPPOSITE
Drawings for four pearl necklaces.

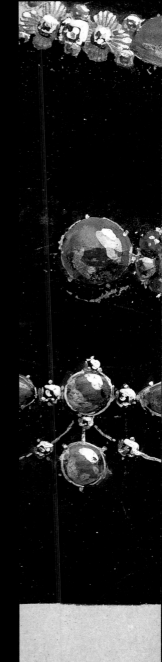

d

ε

OPPOSITE AND ABOVE
Pearl jewelry drawings circa 1875
by the unnamed designer from
Paris. The brooches have the pearl
cascades and garlands fashionable in
Paris in the 1860s. The necklace's
pendant follows the American taste
for star shapes.

As recounted by George Frederick Kunz—Tiffany's legendary gemologist from 1879 to 1932—in his definitive work on pearls *The Book of the Pearl* (originally published by the Century Co., New York, in 1908):

A shoemaker named David Howell, who lived on the outskirts of Paterson, occasionally relieved the monotony of his trade by a fishing excursion to some neighboring stream, where he would usually collect a "mess" of mussels. Returning from one of these visits to Notch Brook in the spring of 1857, the mussels were fried with the usual abundance of grease and heat. After this preparation, one of them was found to contain a large round pearl weighing "nearly 400 grains," which possibly might have proven the finest of modern times, had not its luster and beauty been destroyed by the heat and grease. Had the pearl been discovered in time, its value might have exceeded $25,000, thus making poor Howell's fried mussels one of the most expensive of suppers.

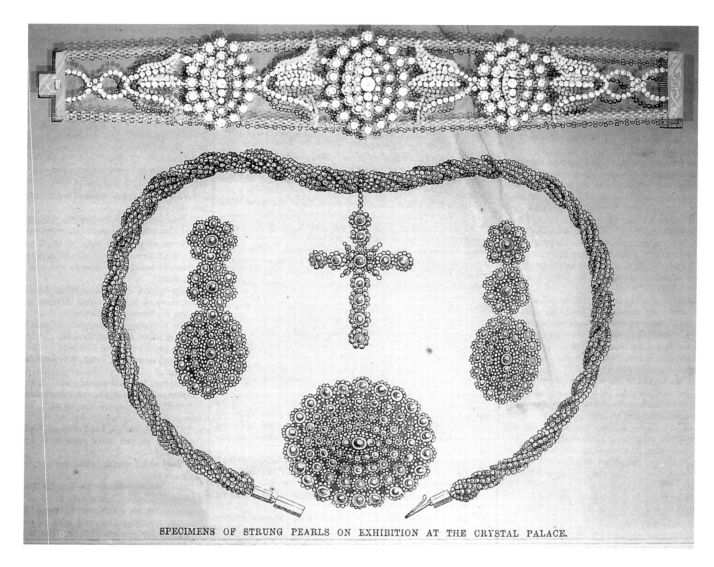

SPECIMENS OF STRUNG PEARLS ON EXHIBITION AT THE CRYSTAL PALACE.

Tiffany & Co.'s seed-pearl parure at the Exhibition of the Industry of All Nations, which opened on July 14, 1853, at New York's Crystal Palace—on the spot that is now Bryant Park. Inspired by similar exhibitions in London in 1851 and Dublin in 1852, it was the first world's fair in America, had over four hundred exhibitors (mostly from the United States), and drew more than a million paid attendees by the time it closed on November 1, 1854 (see pages 58 and 62). Illustration from *Gleason's Pictorial Drawing-Room Companion*, Boston, December 24, 1853.

Circa 1870 seed-pearl bracelet, necklace, and earrings in their original case from Tiffany's Union Square store.

LEFT
Elaborate seed-pearl necklace, probably made around the time of the 1870 opening of Tiffany's Union Square store.

OPPOSITE
Seed-pearl brooch and earrings given to Ella Brooks Carter when she married Charles Warren Cram on April 29, 1869.

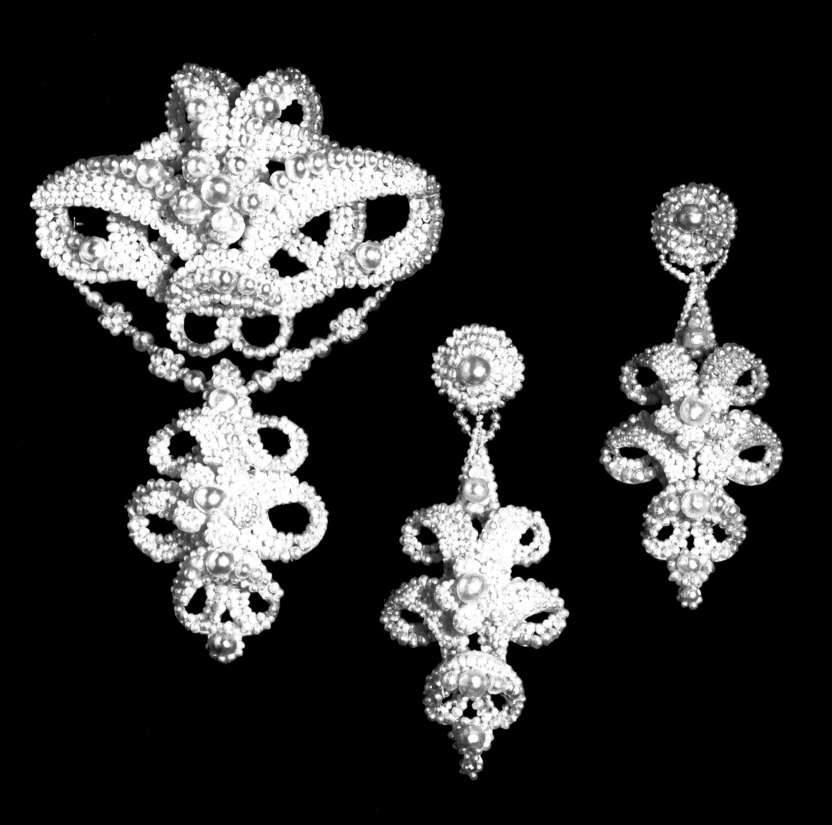

Hoping to duplicate his wonderful find, Howell collected and searched other mussels, and his example was followed by several of his neighbors. Within a few days a magnificent pink pearl was found by a Paterson carpenter named Jacob Quakenbush. This weighed ninety-three grains, and was bought by the late Charles L. Tiffany for Messrs. Tiffany & Co., New York City for $1500. Mr. Tiffany later described with much interest the feelings he experienced after making the purchase. Said he: "Here this man finds a pearl within seventeen miles of our place of business! What if thousands should be found, and many perhaps finer than this one! However, we risked buying the pearl, and as no one in New York seemed interested in it, we sent it to our Paris house for sale, and a French gem dealer offered for it a very large advance on the original price, paying 12,500 francs." From this dealer it passed into the possession of the young and beautiful Empress Eugénie, from whom and from its great luster it derived the name "the Queen Pearl."

OPPOSITE

Gold-and-pearl cuff bracelet in the original Tiffany box, marked "Grand Prix Exposition Universelle 1878." The heavy, matte 18-karat gold is lightened by pearl and diamond "barrettes." The rather English style and the geometrical and "industrial" motifs are typical of the designs of Félix Duval, who may well have made this bracelet for Tiffany's Paris branch. Background photo: The Grotto and the Champs de Mars Palace at the 1878 Paris Exposition.

RIGHT

Above: Drawing for a coral-and-pearl-shell brooch by Tiffany's as-yet-unnamed designer from Paris. Below: A similar late nineteenth-century brooch.

After the fall of Napoléon III, the former empress put the pearl up for auction, along with other personal jewelry, at Christie's in London on June 24, 1872. It was then purchased by Otto von Bismarck's cousin Count Henckel von Donnersmarck, who gave it to his wife, a notorious Russian-born courtesan known as La Païva, whose palatial Paris house on the Champs-Elysées, with its ballroom ceiling by Paul Baudry, was dubbed "the Louvre of prostitution" by the Goncourt brothers. The pearl subsequently dropped out of sight. However, in 1927 a Mr. Fischer of California wrote Tiffany gemologist George F. Kunz that he had seen it worn by the queen of Saxony in 1911 and that the king had once told him he bought it from Donnersmarck for a "very large sum." It has since disappeared from view.

LEFT
Design for a diamond cloverleaf-motif pendant with a central pearl and a pearl drop by Tiffany's unnamed designer from Paris. Late-nineteenth-century clover pendants were often set with white, pink, or gray pearls.

RIGHT
Drawing for a starburst brooch centered by a gray pearl, intended for the Chicago World's Columbian Exposition in 1893.

Diamond crescent pendant with a black Tahitian cultured pearl drop, designed in 2005 in the style of the 1870s. The fashion for crescent jewelry was launched by Empress Eugénie when she wore a crescent with a 42-carat diamond in her hair to receive the pasha of Egypt on his visit to Paris in 1867. Eugénie wore it again when she opened the Suez Canal in 1868.

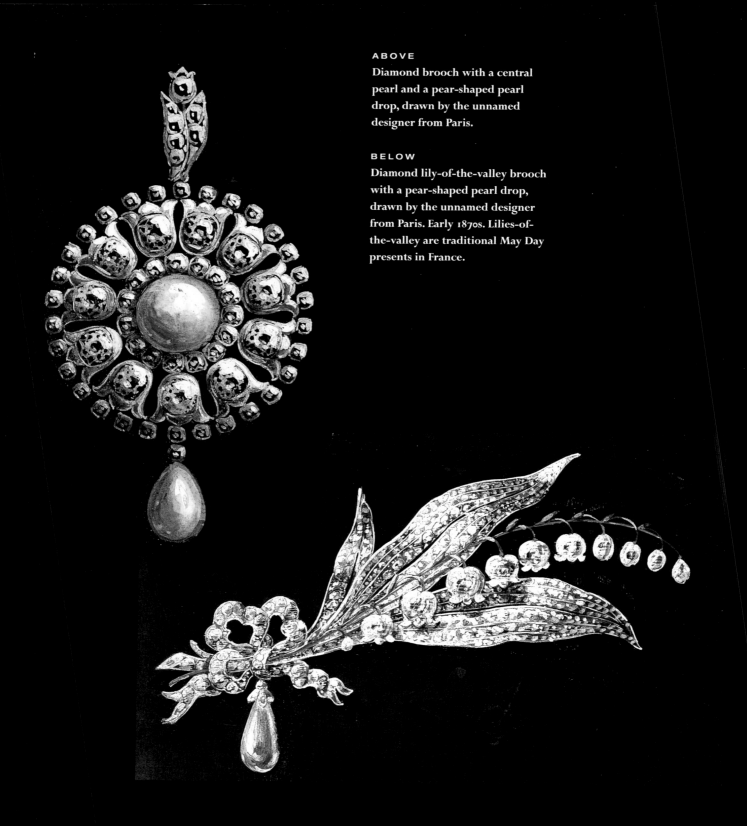

Greek-revival conch pearl
and filigree-bar brooch from
the 1870s. Conch pearl jewelry
became fashionable after leading
Paris jeweler Oscar Massin
(who occasionally provided
designs to Tiffany's) displayed
pink pearl jewelry at the 1867
Paris Exposition.

The purchase and sale of "the Queen Pearl" was far from Tiffany's first adventure in the glorious world of pearls. The earliest piece of jewelry in Tiffany's archival collections is a miniature portrait brooch whose oval gold frame is ornamented with twenty-four white natural pearls and with an 1843 inscription on its backing. The brooch is probably part of Tiffany's first jewelry collection, offered to the public in 1842.

Pearls enjoyed a prominence at Tiffany's to the point that at the first American world's fair, the New York Crystal Palace Exhibition of 1853, the central attraction of Tiffany's jewelry exhibit was an elaborate parure of pearls of modest size but of fine quality.

Gleason's Pictorial Drawing-room Companion, published in Boston on Christmas Eve 1853, described and illustrated the jewels:

"PEARL WORK"

In the case of Tiffany & Co., on exhibition in the Crystal Palace, New York, there are some beautiful specimens of strung pearl work—a necklace, bracelet, cross, etc.—which we have had drawn and present on this page. This style of ornament for the ball-room is exceedingly chaste and effective, and is probably the most becoming jewelry that a lady can wear. In olden times it was very fashionable, and is now being rapidly revived by the adoption of the ladies. Nothing, to our taste, is more refined and beautiful than such ornaments. We do not affect colors: they give a cheap effect at all times, and deteriorate the finest complexion, while pure white is unequalled in appropriateness and delicate beauty under all and every circumstance of full dress. We observe by our foreign files that the Empress Eugénie, wife of the present ruler of France, has a weakness for jet ornaments, just the reverse of these in effect and color, but her taste is questionable, at least, so it seems to us. The idea of putting ornaments into mourning is absurd; either wear them with the legitimate color of ornaments, or else discard them altogether. In England, and on the continent, we understand that pearls are being generally adopted. They stand next to the diamond in cost and real beauty; indeed we have seen a pearl that costs more than any diamond we have happened to see. Large and clear pearls are scarcer than large diamonds.

(*Gleason's* report was accurate except for the gibe at the new empress of France, whose collections of black pearls—of which she was extremely

Foreground: Pearl-and-diamond locket from the 1870s. Background: Locket designs from the same period. Clockwise from top left: Renaissance revival, Greek revival, Japanesque, and Louis XV revival.

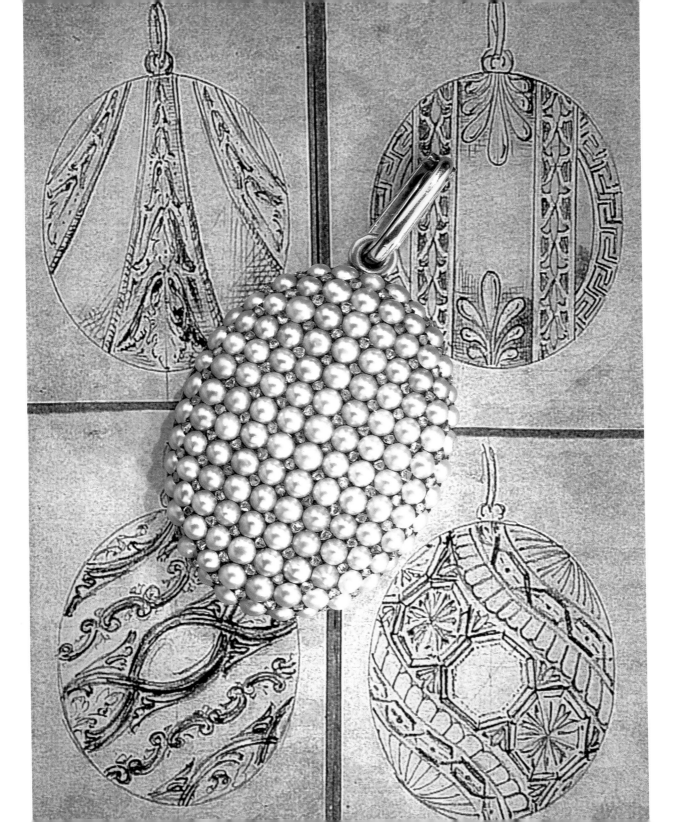

OPPOSITE AND RIGHT
Circa 1880 pearl-and-
diamond pendant and brooch
designs by the unnamed
designer from Paris.

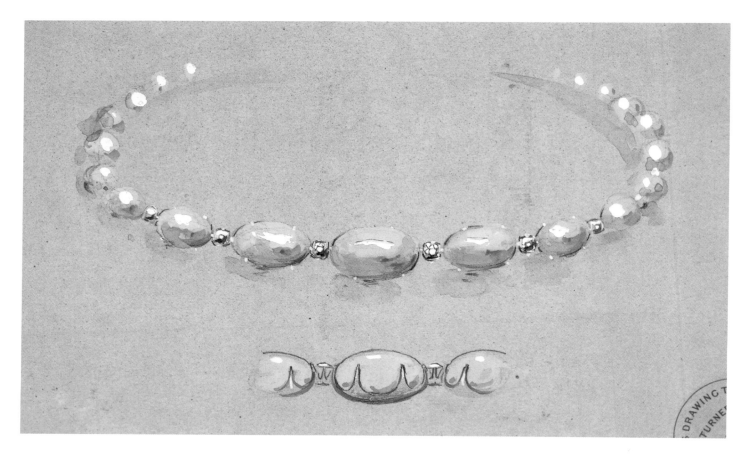

fond—had curiously been mistaken for strings of jet beads. Eugénie's favorite jewel in 1855 was, despite *Gleason's* views, a dazzling nine-inch-long Louis XVI–style corsage ornament made by Gabriel Lemonnier, of cascading diamond leaves and diamond-and-pearl swags with impressively large pendant white pearls, one weighing 337 grains.)

In 1861 President-elect Abraham Lincoln spent a modest $530 at the 550 Broadway Tiffany's store for a gold and seed-pearl parure of earrings, a necklace, a brooch, and pair of bracelets for his wife, Mary Todd Lincoln, to wear to their inaugural ball on March 20, 1861. The price was modest, but Mrs. Lincoln's Tiffany pearls undoubtedly did much to build the already great popularity pearls enjoyed in mid-nineteenth-century America.

Two years later, in the most publicized wedding of the time, Miss Kate Chase, the eldest daughter of President Lincoln's secretary of the treasury (later chief justice of the United States), Salmon P. Chase, married Senator

ABOVE
Circa 1876 design for a necklace of pink conch pearls spaced with diamonds.

OPPOSITE
Floral brooch of conch pearls and diamonds based on a circa 1890 design by Paulding Farnham, 1999.

and former governor William Sprague of Rhode Island. Tiffany & Co. provided the bride's splendid wedding jewels—naturally made from pearls.

President Lincoln, Secretary of State Seward, and other members of Lincoln's cabinet attended the November 12, 1863 wedding, which took place at 8:30 p.m. at the residence of the bride's father at the corner of Sixth and B Streets in the capital.

Harper's Weekly illustrated the Tiffany pearl parure in its November 28 issue and described it in detail:

> No similar event has created so lively a sensation in the fashionable world as that upon which the beautiful ornaments illustrated in the accompanying cut were worn—the marriage of Senator and ex-Governor Sprague, of Rhode Island, to Miss Kate, eldest daughter of the Secretary of the Treasury. The articles engraved are the Tiara, Bracelet, and Earrings of the bridal parure. The material of which they were composed is pearls and diamonds. The Tiara, it will be observed, is especially rich and artistic—a combination of intrinsic and aesthetic features not invariably attained. In addition to such desirable qualities it has likewise a curiously-achieved adaptedness which is not obvious from the sketch. The reader will note the base line of rare pearls; but he does not know, until advised of the fact, that this Orient stream can be diverted from its golden strand and made to encircle the fair neck of its possessor. The zenith itself — "the true lover's knot" of brilliants supporting the mammoth, arrow-riven, heart-shaped pearl—only retains its place at the will of the wearer; the cunning mechanism of the goldsmith having so established its relations to the hidden frame-work, that with the word *presto* it is detached, and, by the addition of a pin and catch, changed into a unique brooch. Thus this beautiful Tiara is either available upon especially grand occasions as an entirety almost unequaled for gracefulness and value—or in each and all of its minor offices as necklace, hair-pins, and brooch. The subjects of the illustration were furnished by Tiffany & Co., of New York. The splendid pearl that constitutes the very front of the Tiara, larger perhaps than any in the country, and in symmetry and rare brilliancy quite warranting the old Latin term *Unio*, has been for some time one of those treasures for the garnering of which that establishment is famous.

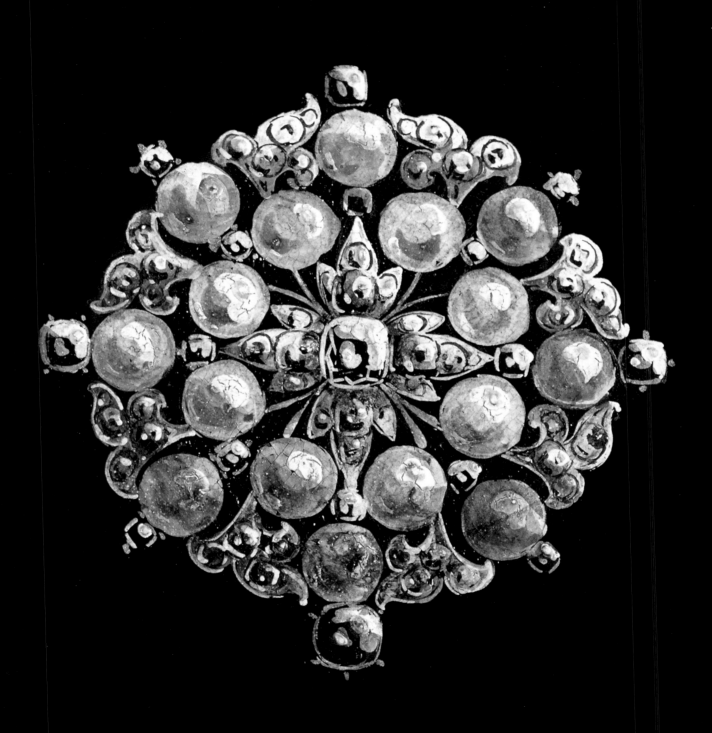

Nine years later the *Brooklyn Eagle* noted on February 28, 1872, that "Messrs. Tiffany & Co. of New York lately sold two of the finest strings of oriental pearls ever disposed of in this country. The price paid for them was $30,000." That was an astonishing sum of money at the time, considering that five years later Tiffany's paid only $18,000 for the 128.54-carat Tiffany Diamond, and had offered the 30-carat Brunswick yellow diamond, set in a large diamond peacock feather, for only $15,000 at the 1876 Philadelphia Centennial Exposition.

Later in the century, George Frederick Kunz devoted a considerable part of his remarkable fifty-three-year tenure as Tiffany's gemologist to bringing the glories of American gemstones and pearls to world prominence, through Tiffany's jewelry displays at the three most important world's fairs: the Paris Exposition of 1889, the Chicago World's Columbian Exposition of 1893, and the Paris Exposition of 1900.

In 1878 large quantities of pearls were discovered in the Little Miami River near Waynesville in southwestern Ohio and collected by a Waynesville banker, Mr. Israel H. Harris. In his first published essay on American pearls, which appeared in the *Jewelers' Weekly* of December 2–9, 1885, Kunz commented on the Harris collection of Miami River pearls:

> One of the finest and best known collections of unio pearls is the
> one belonging to Mr. Israel H. Harris, of Waynesville, O., who
> has for many years purchased and collected everything of value
> in his section of the state of Ohio, where some of the finest
> American pearls have been found. He has a large variety of all
> the oddities and also a fine lot of the good pearls.

The Harris collection had received press attention earlier in Boston's the *Commerical Advertiser* in a feature from April 1879 titled "Pearl Fisheries of Miami":

> Mr. Harris has made a very large and fine collection. From the seed
> pearl to those the size of a pea are included. The luster is exquisite.
> As Mr. Harris held [the pearls] to the light, all the tints of the rain-
> bow were delicately reflected. The changeful opalescent light is like
> sunshine on frost and lovely beyond any description, for the effect
> of pearls seen in masses is enhanced from the effect *à la solitaire*.
> As a little specimen of the way pearls go in the market may be

Paulding Farnham's grandly scaled corsage ornament of conch pearls and diamonds, circa 1890. Its drawing is below.

68

Popular actress Edith Kingdon married George J. Gould, eldest son of "robber baron" Jay Gould, in 1886. Left: Edith Gould's circa 1890 photograph shows her hourglass figure and a fortune in Tiffany pearls, including a pearl tiara, a pearl-and-diamond stomacher, and a sixty-inch "double opera" pearl strand. In 1923 her estate's appraisal included a rope of 90 pearls weighing a total of 1,252 grains, valued at $127,000; a necklace of 51 pearls, 1,326 grains, $105,000; a rope of 187 pearls, 1,700 grains, $85,000; and a four-strand pearl sautoir, 336 pearls, 1,288 grains, $32,000. In today's dollars their total appraised value amounts to about $4 million. Right: collage of photographs of Edith Gould and pearl and diamond jewelry from Tiffany's.

L' EXPOSITION
DE
PARIS 1889

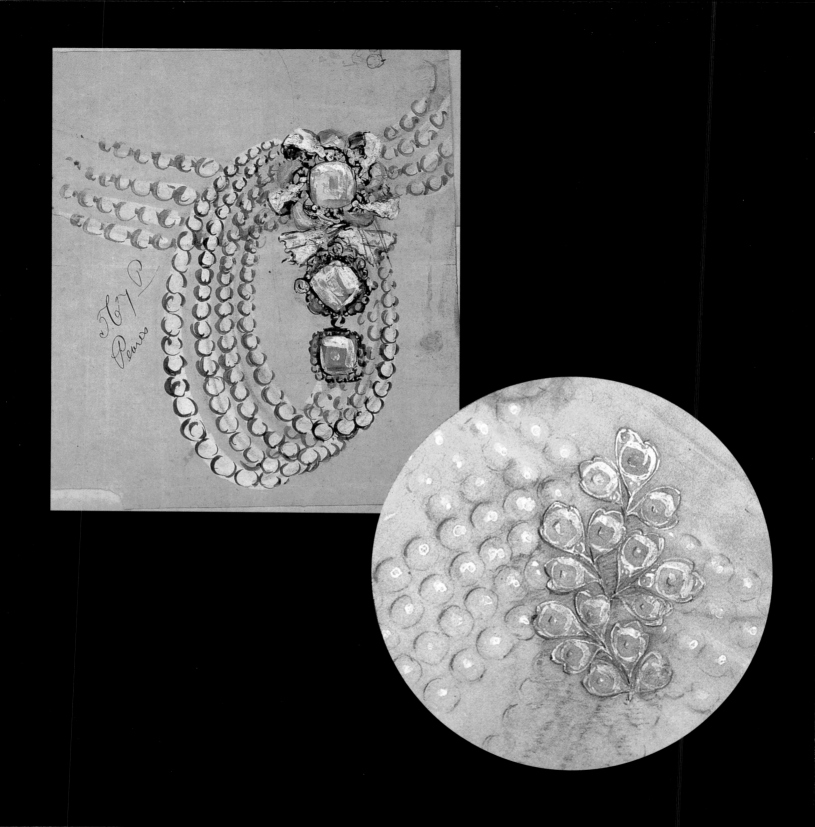

instanced, the Everhart pearl, found in the Miami River here, was sold to Tiffany, in New York, for $100. The Tiffanys sold it to a party in France for $1,000, bought it back for $1,500; and made a final sale of it for $2,800.

The pearls of the little Miami region are of a soft, sky-blue, pink, golden-tinged and iron color, with specimens that show a pure type of each and others that are a blending of all. The colors, of course, are not solid, but exquisite tints and shades, changing with the angle of refracted light. The size ranges from that of a mustard seed to the size of a bullet.

The collection was sold in 1888. Kunz bought many of the finer pearls, and they were made into brooches—some based on American Indian designs—by the company's brilliant twenty-nine-year-old designer Paulding Farnham, for Tiffany's display at the Paris 1889 Exposition. Two were illustrated in the *Jewelers' Weekly* of June 6, 1889, which commented:

A brooch, perhaps 2½ inches in diameter, is composed of 103 pearls of varying size and six clusters of colored stones. Each cluster is formed of one large central gem with twelve smaller ones around it. Alternate smaller clusters add a charming effect to the whole and aid in rendering this brooch one of the most elegant jewels in the entire exhibit. A brooch of Miami Valley pearls, set in an enameled gold mounting in imitation of the basket work of the Alaska Indians, is a strictly American jewel. It contains 175 pearls, that in the center being a very large one. There is a neat setting of diamonds about the center pearl and along the curved arms of the design. The brooch is valued at $650. The selection of pearls has been made by a connoisseur. Only a connoisseur could match them as they are matched in numerous pieces of elaborate jewelry. Many of them, nearly all in fact, are gems of American origin.

There was a spectacular brooch made up of eight black American pearls. The Paris *Herald* reported that "its largest pearl weighed eighty grains, having come from the Gulf of California and valued at 140,000 francs ($28,000)." The American pearls shown by Tiffany & Co. at the 1889 exposition were as a group spectacular and won the company the gold medal for North American pearls.

Elizabeth of Bohemia (1596–1662) wearing what were later to be known as the "Hanoverian Pearls" in her circa 1627 portrait by Daniel Mytens. Elizabeth Stuart was the only surviving daughter of James I of England, who gave her the pearls in 1613 when she married Frederick V, Elector Palatine (1596–1632). In 1658, when their daughter Sophia (1630–1714) married Ernst August, Duke of Brunswick-Lüneberg (and Elector of Hanover from 1692), Elizabeth gave Sophia the pearls her father had given her. The pearls returned to England when Ernst August and Sophia's son George (1660–1727) succeeded as King George I in 1714.

Left: Illustration from *Jewelers' Weekly* of the four-strand necklace with an emerald clasp shown at the 1889 Paris Exposition. The loop of this necklace was probably based on the loop of Elizabeth of Bohemia's necklace in Daniel Mytens's portrait (left).
Right: Archival photograph of the necklace.

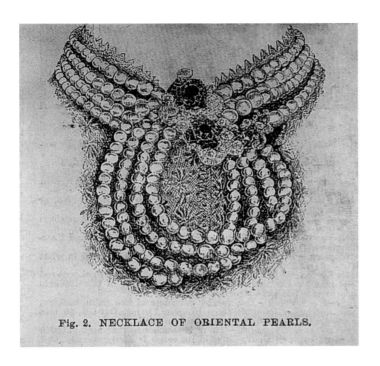

Fig. 2. NECKLACE OF ORIENTAL PEARLS.

Tiffany & Co. naturally showed fine oriental pearls as well, as duly noted by the *Jewelers' Weekly*:

A pearl necklace or collarette is one of the most valuable as well as most beautiful pieces in the exhibit. It consists of four strands of whole pearls. They are oriental gems, 356 in number, and weigh no less than 2,228 grains. The strands are sufficiently long to encircle the neck of the wearer and form a graceful loop in front, as shown in the illustration. The loop is caught up by a clasp composed of five elegant large emeralds, the mountings of which are set with diamonds. The value of this necklace and emerald clasp is $30,000.

The design of this necklace with its "graceful" looped front bears a curious and strong resemblance to the fashion affected by Elizabeth of Bohemia in her state portrait by Daniel Mytens, where four strands of the "Hanoverian" pearls are looped in front and held by a jeweled clasp. Illustrations of this portrait of the seventeenth century's Queen of Hearts (as she was sometimes called) could well have attracted the young Paulding Farnham's attention.

LEFT
Farnham's preliminary sketch for the hexagonal pendant brooch shown below.

BELOW
Hexagonal green-and-yellow enamel pendant brooch with diamonds and American pearls, designed by Paulding Farnham for the 1889 Paris Exposition.

Although in 1889 $30,000 was a remarkable sum to pay for a four-strand necklace of 356 oriental pearls (weighing 2,228 grains), two years later, another four-strand necklace, of 282 pearls weighing 3,441 grains, sold at Tiffany's for an estimated $50,000. Those pearls had been purchased on May 18, 1887, at the Ministry of Finance's public auction of the French crown jewels, where Tiffany & Co. acquired about one-third of the lots offered (more than any other buyer). Lot 40 was the former empress Eugénie's eight-strand pearl necklace; and, to again put into perspective the esteem in which pearls were held relative to diamonds, Tiffany's paid 180,300 francs ($36,060) for four of the eight strands—an almost identical sum to that paid for the most spectacular jewel of the sale, Eugénie's necklace of four diamond rivières consisting of 220 brilliants weighing 360 carats plus 9½ carats of diamonds in the clasp. The price paid was 183,000 francs ($36,600) or only $540 more than for one-half of Eugénie's pearl necklace.

Between the May 1887 sale of the French crown jewels, the Paris Exposition of 1889, and the Chicago World's Columbian Exposition of 1893,

Archival photograph of the "Hupa" brooch of diamonds and pearls from the Little Miami River in Ohio, designed by Paulding Farnham for the 1889 Paris Exposition. Note the gold zigzags between the reverse-curved arms. Tiffany's catalog listed it as follows: "Brooch. Shaped after the decoration of basket work of the Hupa Indians, California." *Jewelers' Weekly* gave a further description: "A brooch of Miami Valley pearls, set in an enameled gold mounting in imitation of the basket work of the Alaska Indians, is a strictly American jewel. It contains 175 pearls, that in the centre being a very large one. There is a neat setting of diamonds about the centre pearl and along the curved arms of the design. The brooch is valued at $650." (June 6, 1889)

RIGHT

Farnham's drawing for a bonbonnière for the 1893 Chicago Exposition, echoing his design for the "Hupa" brooch (opposite).

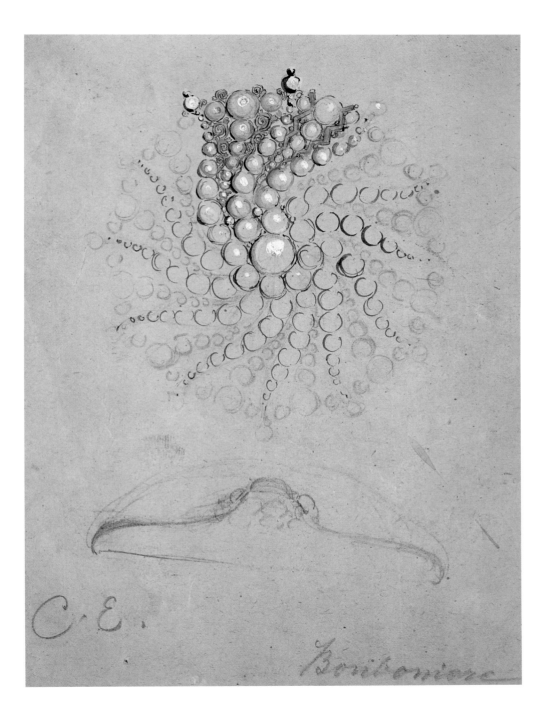

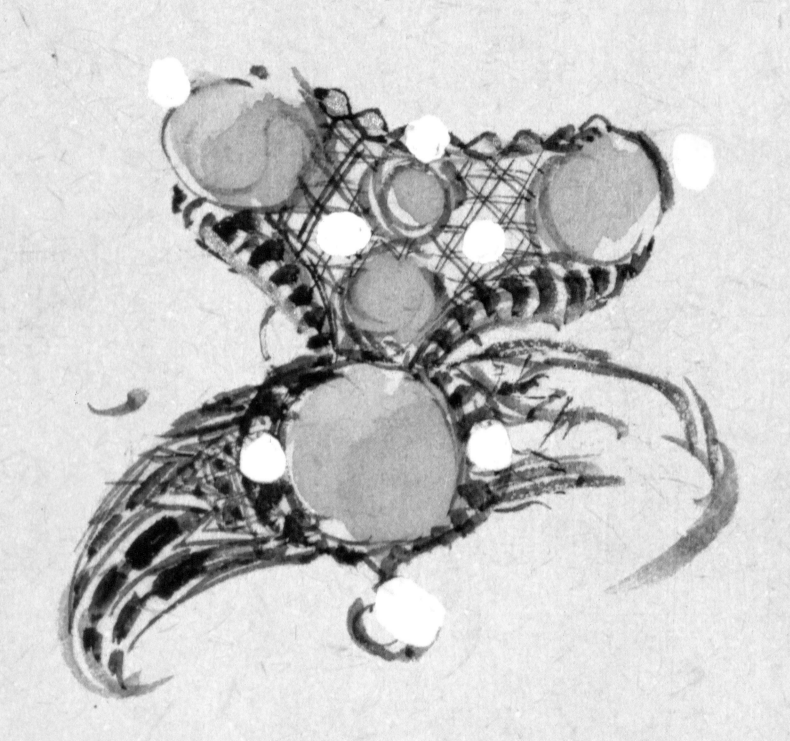

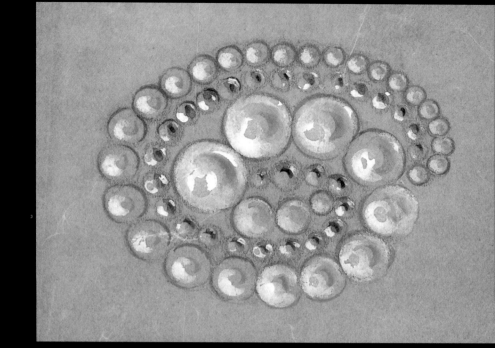

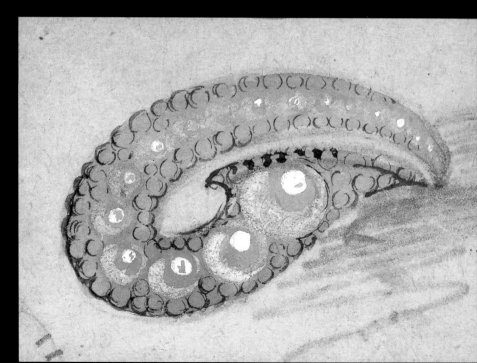

Paulding Farnham's study for
an American Indian–style
ring shown at the 1889 Paris
Exposition; it was listed as
"pink pearl from the Miami
River, Ohio and brilliants from
Brazil, South America."

Farnham's drawing for a brooch
of fifty-five pearls shown at the
1889 Paris Exposition.

Farnham's study for a diamond-
and-American–pearl brooch
shown at the 1889 Paris Exposition.

there was a tremendous increase in the value of fine pearls—commented upon at length and in minute detail in the report made to the French Ministry of Commerce in 1894 by France's representatives at the Chicago exposition.

After having noted the 128.54-carat Tiffany Diamond as being 23¾ carats larger than Queen Victoria's celebrated "Kohinoor," but priced at only 500,000 francs ($100,000), the report lists the astonishing prices of Tiffany pearls shown in Chicago.

One strand of 38 pearls, 1,064 grains, of a value of $200,000 (1 million francs), which puts each pearl at 26,315 francs and the grain at about 940 francs ($188). It's true that the strand is marvelous. Another strand of 44 pearls, 964¾ grains is at 500,000 francs ($100,000), and a strand of 52 pearls weighing 1,145½ grains is at 425,000 francs ($85,000). Another necklace of three strands—equally very beautiful—is made up of 159 pearls and weighs 2,038 grains.

These prices are reassuring and certainly don't indicate a tendance towards devaluation.

The *Jewelers' Review* of November 1893 commented, "A fortune is represented in three strands of truly remarkable pearls. It took many years of even Tiffany & Company's unequalled resources to collect them, and for evenness, tone and perfection no such collection has ever been seen."

As in Paris in 1889, Tiffany's jewelry displays offered fine American pearls at far less than $188 per grain. There were three featured brooches (nos. 12, 20, and 39 in Tiffany's catalog) of Wisconsin purple pearls: one with green enamel and diamonds; another with Maine tourmalines; and another with yellow enamel and diamonds. There was a "Mistletoe" pin of American pearls with emerald leaves. To underscore the Americanness of the pearls, four jewels had American Indian themes, which included tomahawks, peace pipes, and buffalo hooves and horns, all studded with American pearls. There was even a "pearl vase" (no. 152) described as "form Greek, body silver, set with American pearls and chased seaweeds." (The pearl-and-seaweed motif would reemerge ten years later in Tiffany art jewelry.)

At the next great world's fair, the Paris Exposition of 1900, Tiffany focused once more on the use of American gemstones and American pearls in its jewelry display (again designed by Paulding Farnham). The

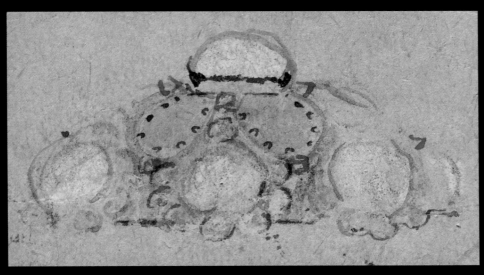

display won the grand prize for jewelry. Oriental pearls were naturally included, notably in the form of a nine-inch-long showstopping corsage ornament made from multicolored pearls of considerable importance and beauty. However, like the Montana sapphires, Maine tourmalines, Arizona garnets, Mexican fire opals, and New Mexican turquoise, the majority of the pearls in Farnham's jewels were the finest examples that Tiffany's gemologist George Frederick Kunz (by then the world's leading expert on pearls and gemstones) could collect. Among the many colorful American pearl brooches was an outstanding jewel of Montana sapphires and eleven superb white American freshwater pearls. There was also a regal pearl, diamond, and enamel necklace of fifteen perfect American pearls with a pendant pearl of remarkable beauty hanging from its central medallion.

At America's celebration of the advent of the twentieth century, the Buffalo Pan-American Exposition of 1901, colorful American baroque pearls were configured into Renaissance-revival jewels by Paulding Farnham to great effect. In their first appearance in Tiffany jewels, these eccentrically shaped but highly lustrous and colorful pearls caught the eye of Louis Comfort Tiffany, America's greatest decorative artist and son of Charles Lewis Tiffany, who had founded Tiffany's in 1837.

LEFT AND OPPOSITE
Archival photograph and drawings of the "Florida Palm" gold-and-enamel brooch, set with ten pink pearls from the Little Miami River and five green Montana sapphires, shown at the 1889 Paris Exposition. The *Jewelers' Weekly* called it "very handsome" and "elegant." George F. Kunz consistently promoted the use of American gems, and Tiffany's display at the 1889 Paris Exposition included "A Collection of Precious and Ornamental Stones of North America" with pearls whose sources ranged from Massachusetts and Minnesota to Key West and Baja California. The collection won a gold medal and was purchased by J. Pierpoint Morgan for New York's American Museum of Natural History.

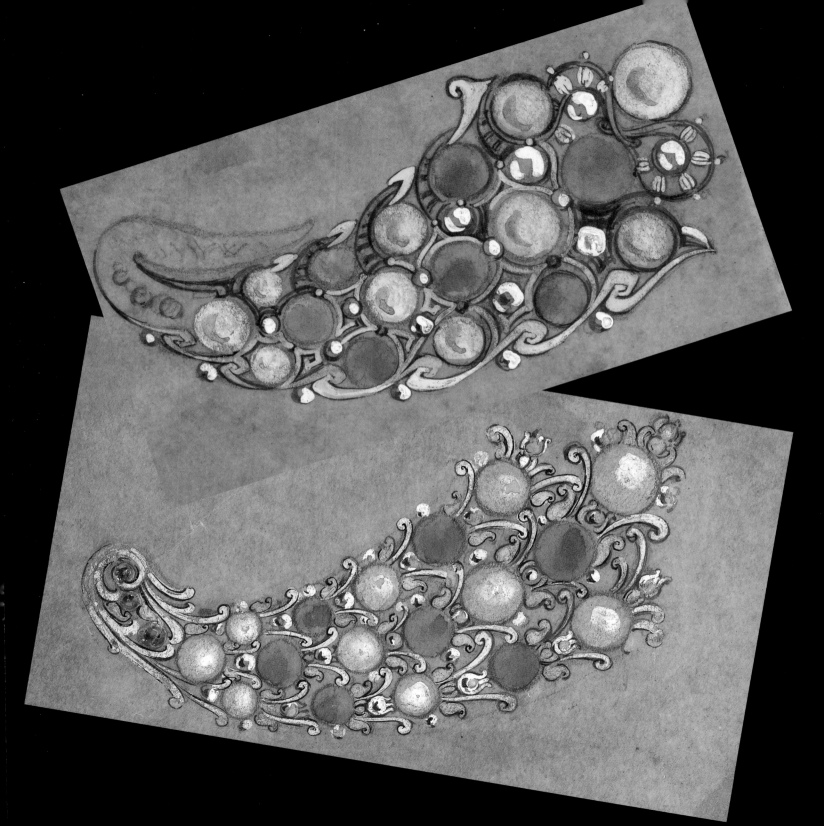

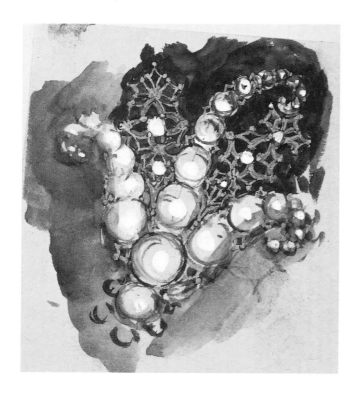 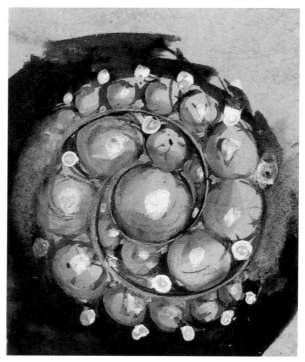

Louis Comfort Tiffany, the year before, had received world acclaim as the unquestioned king of art nouveau glass for his dazzling displays at the 1900 Paris Exposition of his iridescent Tiffany "Favrile" glass vases, glass mosaics, leaded stained-glass lamps, enamel wares, and stained-glass windows. The irregular and colorful pearlescent surfaces of the baroque American pearls shown by his father's company in Buffalo in 1901 had close and obvious affinities to the irregular and colorful iridescent surfaces of his own Favrile glass.

It therefore came as no surprise that the following year, shortly after Louis Comfort Tiffany inherited control of Tiffany & Co., he began for the first time to turn his prodigious imagination and design genius to jewelry design, and that in his initial designs there was great favor shown toward American freshwater baroque pearls, supplied to him by their champion, George Frederick Kunz.

Louis Comfort Tiffany almost never used precious gems in his jewelry. His focus was on the aesthetic excitement his designs produced, and he showed an almost complete disinterest in the intrinsic value of the materials

LEFT
Farnham's sketch for an Orientalist pearl jewel, possibly an aigrette, to be shown at the 1889 Paris Exposition.

RIGHT
Farnham's circa 1889 design for a pearl, gold, and diamond brooch with a spiral typical of American Indian ceramic designs.

Farnham's alternate designs for the collar of the lace necklace shown at the 1889 Paris Exposition. *Jewelers' Weekly* described the finished piece as follows: "A necklace of beautiful tracing of diamonds, representing a piece of lace, fastened in front by a cluster composed of a very large pearl, weighing 99 grains surrounded by large diamonds, from which drops a delicate spray of diamond lace work . . . [It] is a very handsome ornament . . . valued at $8,000." (June 6, 1889)

Order 1291

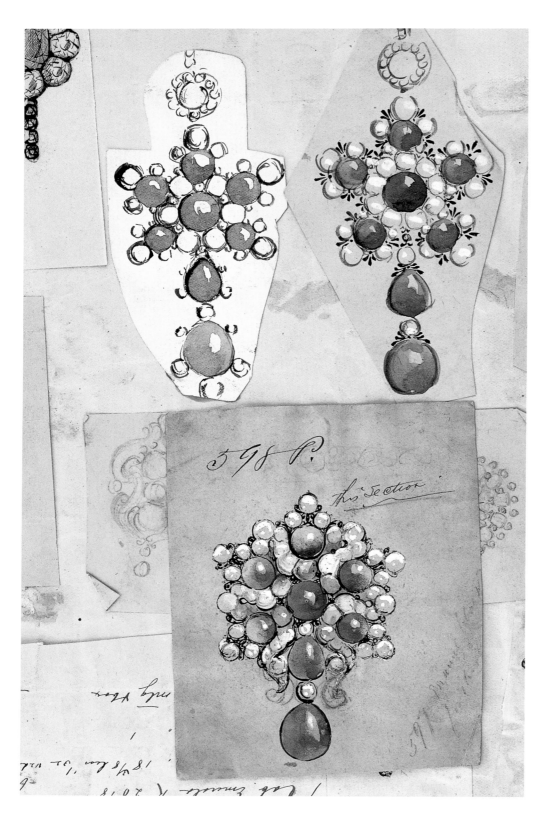

Farnham's preliminary sketches and archival photograph of the black-pearl pendant shown at the 1889 Paris Exposition. George Frederick Kunz mentioned its fifty-grain drop in his article on American pearls that appeared in the *Jewelers' Weekly,* December 2, 1885: "Perhaps the greatest pearl fishery in America is the one at La Paz, lower [Baja] California. The pearls vary in color from pure white, through all the shades of white, gray, and brown, to black; the latter having become so fashionable of late years that their value has increased as much as ten-fold. . . . One black pearl, weighing fifty grains, was valued at $8,000."

Single-strand graduated pearl necklaces. Background top: Necklace of fifty-three graduated pearls, priced at $600,000, shown at the 1939–1940 New York World's Fair. Background bottom: Drawing for a necklace for the 1889 Paris Exposition; its sixty-one oriental pearls were graduated from 14 millimeters at center front to 8 millimeters at back. Foreground: Important necklace of eighty-three pearls made about 1939–1940.

OPPOSITE
Drawing by Tiffany's unnamed
designer from Paris for a fleur-
de-lis diamond brooch with a
yellow sapphire, a blue sapphire,
three pearls, and an oval pearl drop.

ABOVE
Drawing by the same designer
for a diamond brooch with a
black pearl drop; it may have
been the same fifty-grain black
pearl used in the pendant shown
on pages 92 and 93.

he employed. Beauty, not cost, was the issue, and American freshwater baroque pearls fit the bill. They were of a very great beauty and a very slight cost.

At the 1901 Buffalo exposition, the French *Revue de la Bijouterie* had noted Tiffany & Co.'s policy of often using less expensive materials to great effect in their designer jewelry collections:

> Going on to Tiffany's jewelry, their display has a very special charac-
> ter. It shows a real effort to discover artistic effects without taking
> into account the importance accorded to jewelry by the value of
> the stones [and pearls] employed. It appears that they seek only to
> elicit a fresh response by their use of decorative stones of American
> origin. This appears to be very American in itself, as Tiffany's has by
> this method created beautiful and artistic jewels which because of
> the stones employed are at affordable prices.

BELOW
Circa 1889 drawing for necklace
of American freshwater pearls and
diamonds, with alternate designs
for pendants.

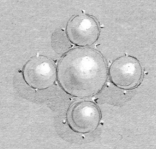

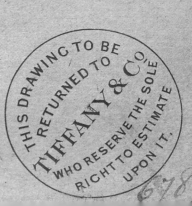

Louis Comfort Tiffany showed his first collection of Tiffany art jewelry at the St. Louis Louisiana Purchase Exposition of 1904, and several pieces featured the beautiful if inexpensive American freshwater pearls provided by George Frederick Kunz.

American baroque pearls remained a staple of Tiffany art-jewelry design, eventually combining with faceted gemstones as the 1920s and the art deco period approached and brought an end to the rich, dark, saturated colors, the organic undulations, and the exoticism of art nouveau.

But the eccentric forms of Kunz's and Louis Comfort Tiffany's colorful baroque freshwater pearls were very soon replaced by an ever-greater thirst for fine white oriental pearls, as the art nouveau period was ended by World War I and the art deco period began.

ABOVE AND OPPOSITE
Posters for the World's Columbian Exposition held in Chicago in 1893, showing the 1,700-foot-long Manufacturers and Liberal Arts Building where Tiffany's exhibit took place.

The art deco period and the "roaring" 1920s were distinguished by ever-accelerating spending, paralleled by ever-accelerating inflation. Oriental pearls were again the jewels of the day, judging from the fashion press as well as from Tiffany's sales records.

On July 15, 1920, Chase National Bank vice president Carl J. Schmidlapp purchased for $292,000 a pearl choker weighing 1,383 grains for his bride, Frances (the granddaughter of James Fenimore Cooper). Chicago's social queen, Mrs. Potter Palmer, paid $150,000 shortly after for a pair of Australian pearl and diamond earrings.

Retailing heir Rodman Wanamaker bought a necklace of eighty-one pearls for 488,700 francs ($97,740) at Tiffany's Paris branch on October 25, 1921. On March 13, 1923, he spent 1,776,320 francs ($355,264) for more pearls. Six weeks later, Anna Gould, Duchess of Talleyrand-Périgord (who ran Rodman Wanamaker a close second as Tiffany's most extravagant jewelry client of the 1920s) bought a hair ornament with two pear-shaped pearls for 188,500 francs ($37,700).

Pearls were the one jewel that no stylish lady could be without. The very rich, especially the newly very rich, bought pearls, pearls, and more pearls.

For the more modestly rich, there were pearls of more modest size and cost, such as the necklace of fifty-five pearls Mrs. Rudyard Kipling bought at Tiffany's London branch in December 1926 for 5,900 pounds ($29,500). However, bigger was better when it came to pearls in high society, if not in literary circles. On July 31, 1925, Mr. Wanamaker bought an opera-length necklace of seventy-nine pearls, again at Tiffany's Paris shop, for 1,144,000 francs ($228,800), and that September he returned for an even larger pearl necklace for 1,522,400 francs ($304,480). Then in November he added four enormous pearls weighing an astonishing 926.96 grains to his collection for 1,098,240 francs ($219,648). On a single Tiffany pearl, only Mrs. Marshall Field outspent him when she bought a 77.50-grain pearl (noted in Tiffany's sales book, "with a crack") for 300,000 francs ($60,000) on October 8, 1924, putting the pearl at $774.19 a grain—possibly a world's record.

This all came to a screeching halt with the stock market crash of 1929. Tiffany & Co.'s personnel records are telling. In May 1930 there were eleven full-time pearl stringers employed at the Fifth Avenue and 37th Street store. By the time the Depression had taken its toll in May 1940, there were only two.

OPPOSITE ABOVE
Farnham's preliminary study for the "Hungarian Brooch" shown at the Chicago Exposition. The finished brooch was described in Tiffany's catalog as "baroque pearl in center, surrounded by seven green tourmalines and small diamonds." The pearl was from Wisconsin, weighed sixty-four grains, and cost $128. The brooch was priced at $400.

OPPOSITE BELOW
Farnham's drawing for a pearl-and-diamond brooch representing a basket of flowers. The design includes three flowers with pearl petals, three pear-shaped pearl drops, and clusters of small golden pearls. A similar brooch was shown at the 1893 Chicago Exposition.

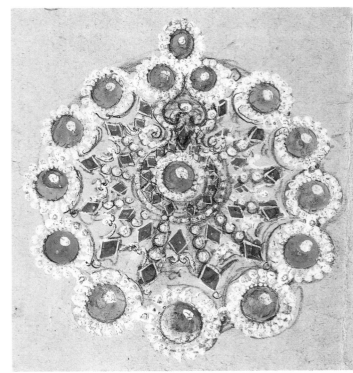

OPPOSITE
Orientalist brooch with a large central pink sapphire, smaller pink sapphires, varicolored pearls, yellow sapphires, diamonds, and demantoids. Designed by Paulding Farnham, circa 1890.

LEFT
Farnham's drawing for the brooch opposite.

RIGHT
Drawing for a pendant brooch shown at the 1893 Chicago Exposition; Tiffany's catalog listed it as follows: "Fancy Brooch. Pink pearls, with emeralds in center."

However, while the sale of strands of pearls in the hundreds of thousands of dollars came to an abrupt halt, their prices did not decline accordingly. Pearl prices at Tiffany's held their own throughout the Great Depression, and pearls retained their first place among jewels when Tiffany & Co.'s flagship store opened at Fifth Avenue and Fifty-seventh Street on Monday, October 21, 1940.

On November 4, 1940, *Time* magazine noted the following among "the toniest United States jewelers' dazzling stock: diamond solitaires up to 20½ carats (price $100,000), pearls (up to $243,000 a string)."

Time's reporter overlooked another, more important Tiffany single-strand pearl necklace of fifty-three exceptionally fine oriental pearls that had just returned from Tiffany's display in the House of Jewels at the 1939–1940 New York World's Fair. That necklace was priced at $600,000, while the Tiffany Diamond had been shown at the fair for a mere $200,000.

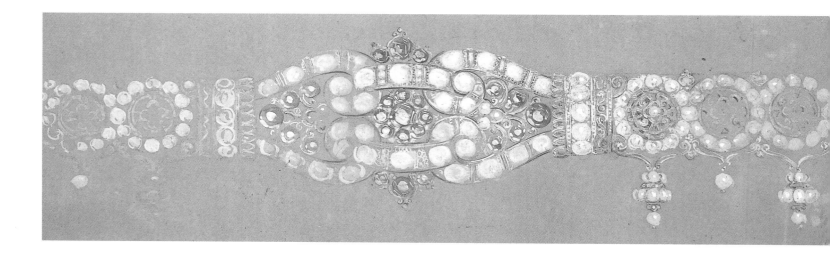

As previously observed, with such stratospheric prices, women of the time turned to fashion jewelry made with imitation pearls, until in the late 1950s the introduction of cultured pearls into the fine-jewelry industry again brought pearls of great quality within the general public's reach.

It was exactly at this turning point in the history of pearls that the father of fashion jewelry, Jean Schlumberger, came to design exclusively for Tiffany & Co., on February 17, 1956.

Jean Schlumberger created the most glamorous jewels of the twentieth century. His fascination with the surrealistic and with the exotic, tropical, and submarine aspects of nature drove him to a desire "to capture the irregularity of the universe," to explore what he termed "the mysterious garden of the imagination," and to create jewels that he and the world saw as "sheer poetry."

Born in 1907 in Mulhouse in eastern France to a wealthy family of textile manufacturers (who would have liked him to pursue a career in banking), Schlumberger was attracted from the start, not to finance or even to textile design (which he briefly pursued) but to the glamorous, fashionable, and artistic world of 1930s Paris. After he left a banking job in Berlin for a post with the Paris art publisher Braun, Schlumberger's charm and imagination quickly catapulted him to the center of French café society and fashion; in 1935, he created his first highly inventive jewels from 120 Dresden porcelain flowers bought at the Paris flea market.

Circa 1890 orientalist designs by Paulding Farnham.

ABOVE
A jeweled belt. At the left Farnham offered the option of pearls rather than sapphires.

OPPOSITE
Brooch of small pearls set in a geometrical pattern. Note Farnham's characteristic infilling of tiny gold triangles.

142.

Flexible

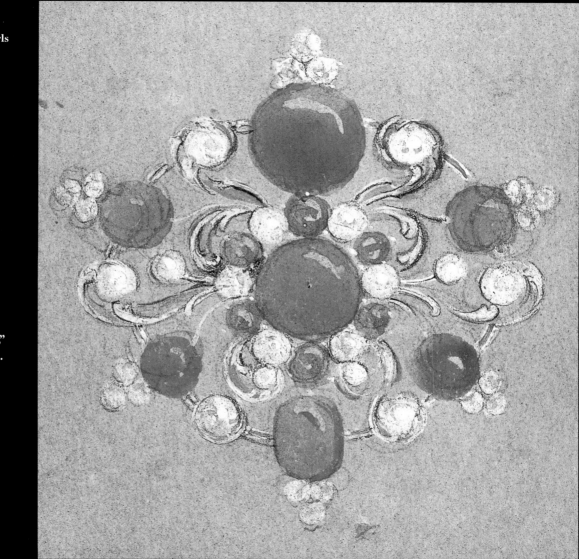

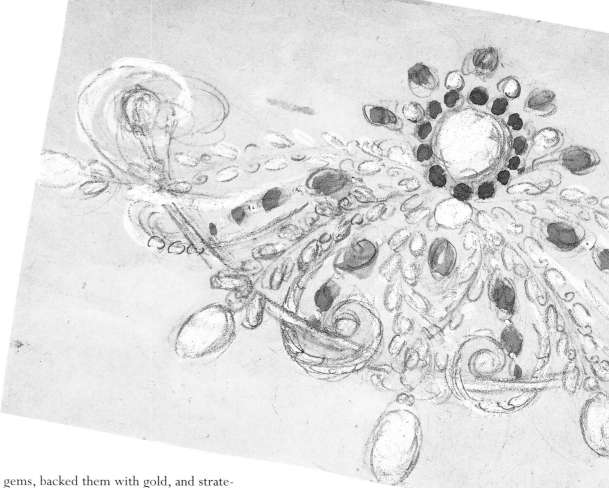

He studded the flowers with gems, backed them with gold, and strategically presented them to several leading Paris socialites, including Singer sewing machine heiress Mrs. Reginald "Daisy" Fellowes, who was also conveniently the Paris correspondent of *Harper's Bazaar.* The porcelain flower jewels quickly came to the attention of that most audacious of fashion designers, Elsa Schiaparelli (for whom Salvador Dalí was already designing, along with three other surrealists, Leonor Fini and the brothers Roberto and Serge Matta).

Schiaparelli at once employed Schlumberger to make buttons with surrealist overtones for her costume collections, of unexpected found objects, including wooden chessmen. He "used the most unbelievable objects," she later commented in her memoirs, "animals, feathers, caricatures, paper weights, chains, locks . . . some were wood, others plastic, but none resembled anything a button should resemble."

Inspired by the asymmetries and idiosyncrasies of the world and using his vocabulary of unexpected materials, Schlumberger soon added to his designs for Schiaparelli some of the first fashion jewelry ever created. He continued to design for her until the outbreak of World War II in 1939.

After serving in the armed forces during the war, Schlumberger came to New York, where he opened his own jewelry business in 1947. No celebrity of the social or fashion worlds of either Paris or New York could be without Schlumberger's ever-so-stylish and whimsical jewels.

Diana Vreeland, the "empress" of twentieth-century fashion and editor in chief of *Harper's Bazaar* and then *Vogue*, commented on the works of Jean Schlumberger in her ever-poetic manner. She described the jewels he created at the start of his career with Schiaparelli: "Chinese pink starfish or a plumed hat of d'Artagnan, speckled pebbles of many colors" and later went on: "He loves the sea and all of its creatures. The creatures of the sea are very special to Schlumberger. As I go back in my memories, I see tiny sea creatures of diamonds and pearls in a watery world of turquoise. A lovely cockleshell. Sea anemones. Seashells, pearly shells, speckled shells."

Schlumberger's love of the idiosyncratic in nature, of exotic sea creatures, and of curious and splendid flowers, coupled with his Parisian wit and elegance, brought Tiffany again into a position of design leadership in the world of jewels; and Tiffany's gem and pearl collections gave Schlumberger the materials to unleash the full range of his fertile and colorful imagination. In the '50s and '60s, Schlumberger's lavish, witty, and unexpected jewels were the pride of Tiffany & Co., and they retain that position today, fifty years later.

His passion for the beauty of the underwater world led him to wholeheartedly embrace a lavish use of cultured pearls in his Tiffany designs, an indulgence he had been denied at the outset of his career in late 1930s Paris, when natural pearls still reigned supreme in fine jewelry and imitation pearls were the poor alternative. The first were too costly for fashion, the second beneath its interest.

The availability of cultured pearls at Tiffany & Co. unleashed a fresh burst of creativity in Schlumberger. Suddenly there were exotic floral brooches of black pearls and yellow diamonds; earrings of baroque pearls with upswept golden "wings"; lavish torsades of white pearls gripped by gold and colored enamel stations; basket rings overflowing with pearls; bracelets bristling with mixed black and white pearls; domed mabe pearls

as earrings bound with gold ropes and punctuated with tiny diamonds; lavish South Sea pearls alternated with pavé diamond "pebbles"; brooches with golden pea pods filled with pearls. With Schlumberger's Tiffany designs, pearls and high fashion finally marched to the same beat.

At the same time, amply scaled South Sea, Tahitian, and Burmese cultured pearls were all the vogue, and women no longer discussed pearls in grains (as they had fine oriental pearls) but in millimeters, beginning with 8-millimeter pearls (about fourteen grains). By the late 1970s the higher reaches of society thought nothing of discussing 14-millimeter pearls (about eighty grains) and even 15-millimeters pearls (about ninety grains). (At 15½ millimeters a pearl weighs over a hundred grains.) Cultured pearls, once so affordable, began to skyrocket in price. The finest Tiffany cultured pearls at these levels were back in the hundreds of thousands of dollars.

Tiffany's 1961–1962 Blue Book catalog offered examples "from the Tiffany collection of cultured pearls distinguished for exceptionally large

LEFT
Silver coffeepot designed by Charles Osborne, circa 1882. It has Osborne's characteristic repoussé-chased "pearling" in spiraling configurations, with actual pearls circling the body below the lid.

RIGHT
John T. Curran designed this seven-inch-tall pearl-studded silver vase for the 1893 World's Columbian Exposition in Chicago. The swirling seaweed shows Curran's affinities with the nascent Art Nouveau movement. This and a similar vase with "old Irish aquamarines" were purchased at the exposition by Berlin's Kunstgewerbemuseum, which still has them in its collection.

BELOW
Silver-gilt, pearl, and enamel
coffee set designed by Paulding
Farnham, 1902–1905.

size, fine color, and luster." There was a double-strand necklace of seventy-four white South Sea pearls, graduated from 7 to 14 millimeters, for $100,000; and a matching ring with a single 14-millimeter pearl atop a dome of small marquise diamonds for $7,500. Had the necklace been made up of only 14-millimeter pearls, its price would have exceeded $350,000.

Burmese cultured pearls were introduced in the 1964–1965 Blue Book with a magnificent graduated strand of twenty-seven pearls, ranging from 10 to 14 millimeters and again priced at $100,000.

The catalog made the case for the subtle perfection of Tiffany's prized new pearls:

Less than ten years ago the waters of the Gulf of Martaban started to yield the largest, most beautiful and now the rarest of cultured pearls. These pearls, which possess pure white color with pink overtones and superb luster, are the result of the unusual environment found only in the waters of this area.

240   Eiffel Tower and River Seine, Paris France.

ABOVE

Stereoscopic view of the 1900 Paris Exposition. The domed United States pavilion, where Tiffany & Co. had its main display, is at far left. Tiffany's also displayed a collection of 731 American pearls in the exposition's Palace of Forestry, Hunting, and Fisheries, across the Seine from the United States pavilion. Like Tiffany's display of American gems at the 1889 Paris Exposition, this collection was assembled by George F. Kunz, won a gold medal, and was purchased for the American Museum of Natural

OPPOSITE

Drawing for a pendant necklace of sixteen American pearls and 167 diamonds, shown at the 1900 Paris Exposition. The drop had a button pearl weighing 25.8 grains and costing $300, and a pear-shaped pearl weighing 52.3 grains and costing $520. The necklace's total cost was $1,912.90; it was priced at $3,500.

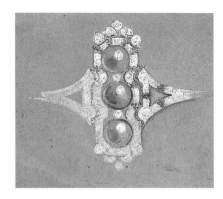

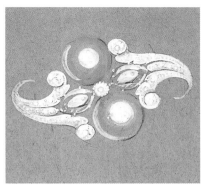

OPPOSITE
Farnham's drawing for an important pearl and diamond ornament intended for the 1900 Paris Exposition; forty-five American pearls (including the central 18.9-grain purple Wisconsin pearl costing $200) were collected for this piece, but it was not made.

RIGHT

Three designs for rings made for the 1900 Paris Exposition. The drawing at upper left shows a ring with three brown pearls from the Cumberland River in Tennessee (costing $808) and fifty-two small diamonds; it was priced at $1,600. The drawing at upper right shows a ring with two pink pearls from the Little Miami River in Ohio, two marquise yellow diamonds, and forty-one small white diamonds; it was priced at $1,000. The drawing below shows a ring with a pink pearl and a white pearl with forty-two small diamonds. Together the two pearls weighed 47.5 grains and cost $475; the ring was priced at $1,350.

Tiffany & Company were able to select the cream of the entire yield. Therefore we are able to offer the largest and finest cultured pearls known to exist today. These are now available at Tiffany & Co. in a number of magnificent necklaces, earrings, and rings.

In the spring of 1963, Burma nationalized the pearl fisheries and production ceased. It is our belief that we may never see pearls of this quality produced again in the foreseeable future.

The final prediction fortunately turned out to be inaccurate, and the 1966–1967 Blue Book offered exceptional pearls from Burma's Gulf of Martaban.

The high-fashion jewelry design that Jean Schlumberger introduced to Paris in the late 1930s and to Tiffany & Co. in 1957 changed the public's taste regarding pearls during the second half of the twentieth century far more than did the acceptance and gradual triumph of fine cultured pearls from the South Seas.

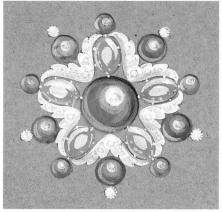
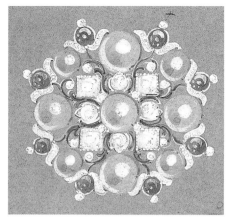
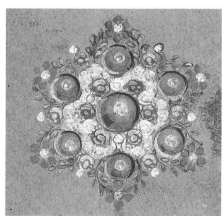

LEFT

Drawings for four pearl brooches shown at the 1900 Paris Exposition. The brooch at upper left was centered by a 31.5-grain American pearl costing $340, ten smaller American pearls, five yellow marquise diamonds, and thirty-nine small white diamonds; the brooch was priced at $2,000. The brooch at upper right had nine American pearls averaging ten grains each, eight green tourmalines, and ninety-two small diamonds; it was priced at $2,000. The brooch at lower left had seven American pearls, twelve green tourmalines, and forty-two small diamonds; it was priced at $900. The brooch at lower right was centered by a 21.1-grain white American pearl costing $422; it also had eight varicolored American pearls and eighty small diamonds; it was priced at $2,000.

OPPOSITE

Drawing for a brooch of eleven pearls, fifteen pink tourmalines, and fifty-seven small diamonds, priced at $900 at the 1900 Paris Exposition. The drawing is signed "Drivet" for jeweler Jacques Michel Drivet. Born in France in 1859, he emigrated to New York in 1886 and joined Tiffany's around 1888 to work on jewelry for the 1889 Paris Exposition.

Like Louis Comfort Tiffany before him, who valued the baroque American pearls and other materials used in his Tiffany art jewelry for their intrinsic beauty rather than for their dollar value, Schlumberger's own witty, whimsical, and ever-so-stylish mixtures of the precious and not so precious opened new avenues for future generations of Tiffany designers. Most notable among those are Angela Cummings, Elsa Peretti, and Paloma Picasso.

In 1972 Tiffany & Co. presented its first collection of jewels by the young Austrian-German designer Angela Cummings. Her lyrical mode in design and her fondness for pastel colors, combined with a love of the beauty she saw everywhere in nature, quickly led her to an extensive use of colored freshwater pearls, baroque pearls, and even mother-of-pearl

Drívet

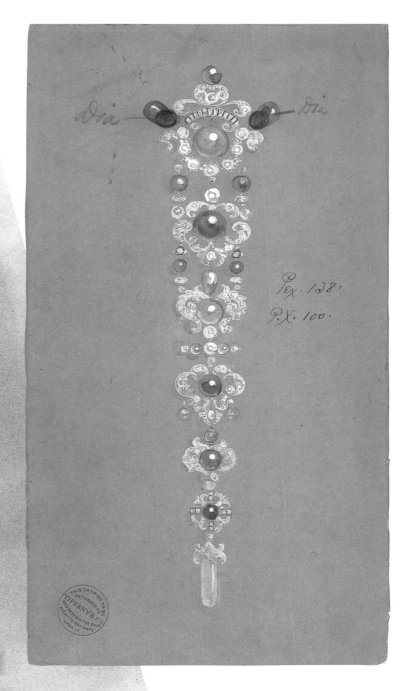

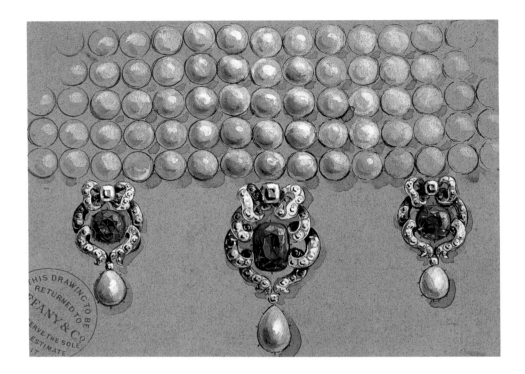

inlays. Often combined with soft-surfaced matte gold, the softly lustrous surfaces of pearls and their subtle, evanescent hues gave her jewels the lilting, romantic, feminine, even confectionary charm of a Strauss waltz or opera—at once stage jewels for *Der Rosenkavalier* and butter-icing cake decorations.

There was always great subtlety in Cummings's combinations of rose, mauve, pink, and gray pearls in opulent thick torsades and gracefully fluid lariats. Even China's humble freshwater "Rice Krispie" pearls and Japan's cockscomb pearl mussel found their place in her popular opera-length multiple-strand necklace with a hammered-gold cushion clasp. The variety of colored pearls, too, was rich in Cummings's jewelry, lending either a festive quality or a quiet beauty in its pastel lyricism.

Then in 1974, Elsa Peretti—who was to become the most successful and the most influential jewelry designer of the last quarter of the twentieth century—joined Tiffany & Co. The absolute perfection of her sculptural, often organic, and always eminently sensual designs would revolutionize contemporary jewelry.

ABOVE
A circa 1900 proposal for a five-strand pearl choker with diamonds, rubies, and pearl drops.

OPPOSITE
Foreground: "Dog collar" choker with twelve strands of pearls and spacers set with diamonds. Chokers were popularized by the Princess of Wales (1844–1925, Queen Alexandra from 1901), whose favorite choker included some of the Hanoverian pearls. Background: An outdoor café at the 1900 Paris Exposition overlooking the Palace of Electricity outlined with five thousand light bulbs.

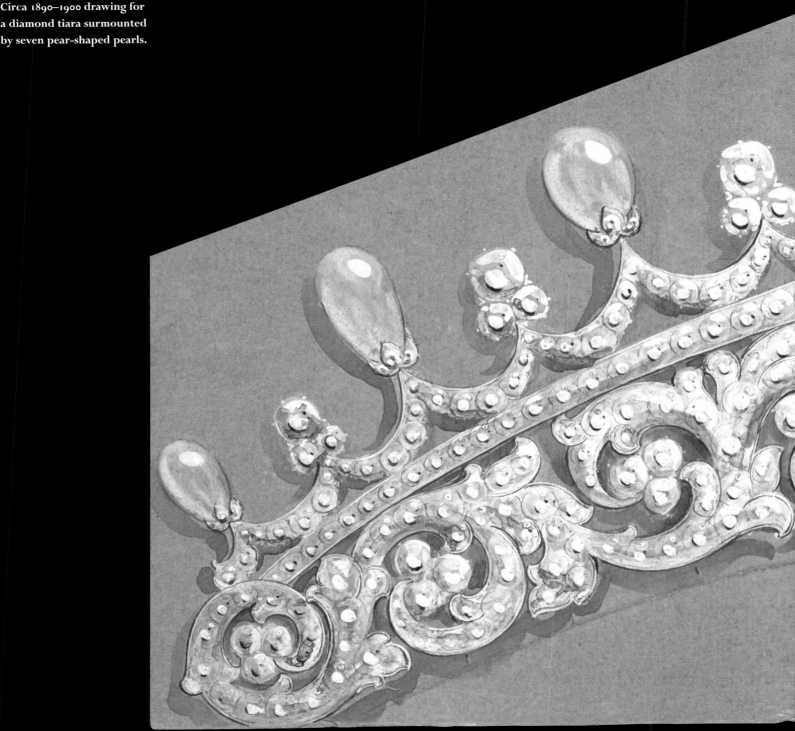

Circa 1890–1900 drawing for
a diamond tiara surmounted
by seven pear-shaped pearls.

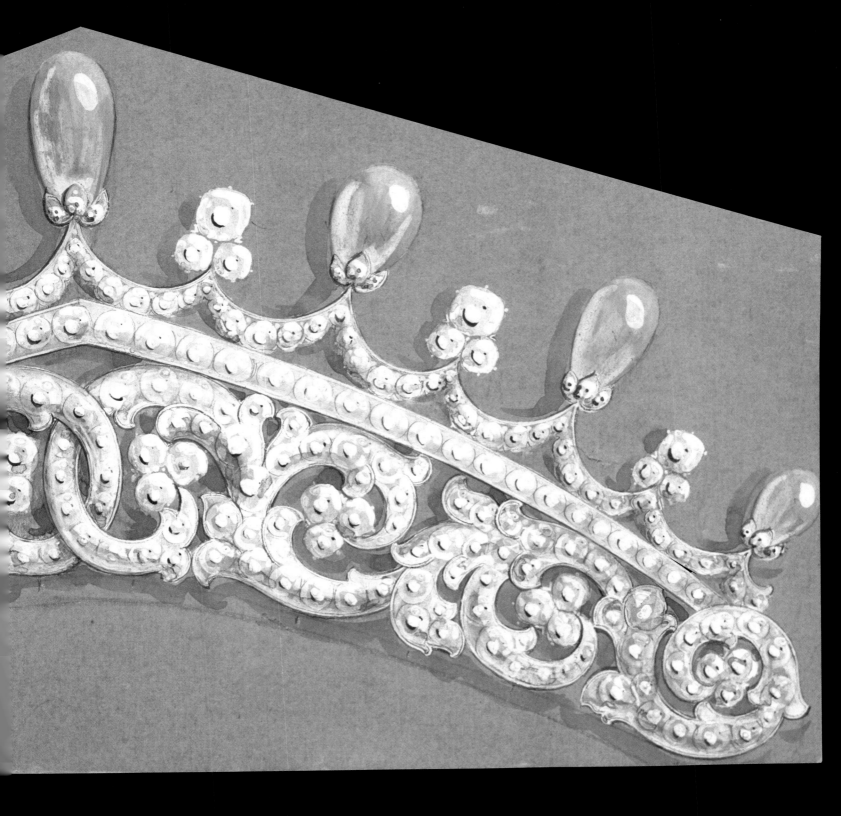

Paulding Farnham's drawing for a brooch of seven large black pearls, seventeen yellow diamonds, and sixteen white diamonds made for the 1900 Paris Exposition. The pearls probably came from La Paz.

Gold-and-platinum brooch with eleven freshwater pearls from Wisconsin and Tennessee, ten Montana sapphires, and 103 diamonds, designed by Paulding Farnham for the 1900 Paris Exhibition.

In 1977, *Newsweek's* April 4 cover story, "Jewelry's New Dazzle," featured Peretti's Tiffany designs.

It all began at staid old Tiffany's, with the arrival of a tempestuous Italian ex-model named Elsa Peretti. Scion of a wealthy Roman family (her father, Ferdinando Peretti, founded and owned Italy's API oil company, the country's second largest) and a star in the New York fashion galaxy, 36-year-old Elsa Peretti is as elegant and unorthodox as the jewelry she designs. Passionate about almost everything, the 5-foot 9-inch Peretti creates a scene wherever she goes. She is also obsessed with her work as a designer and dedicated to perfection. And this personal touch, her love of nature, her infallible taste—have resulted in a whole new kind of jewelry meant to feel as good as it looks. "Since Elsa," says Henri Bendel president Geraldine Stutz, "nothing in jewelry has been the same."

What Peretti had was a whole new idea of what jewelry should be: more design than decoration, with simple, softer, sculptural

LEFT
Farnham's drawing for an orientalist buckle for the 1900 Paris Exposition. As completed, it was set with twenty-three American pearls, six turquoises, eight rubies, and twenty-five rose-cut diamonds; the central pearl weighed 14¼ grains. The buckle was priced at $1,150.

RIGHT
Farnham's circa 1900 design for a corsage ornament of diamonds and pearls of various shapes and colors.

OPPOSITE
Farnham's circa 1900 diamond bow brooch with varicolored pearls and gemstones.

TIFFANY & CO. EXHIBIT
PAN-AMERICAN EXPOSITION
BUFFALO 1901

NEG. NO. 2417

Archival photograph of a corsage
ornament centered by a large rose
diamond, designed by Farnham for
the Pan-American Exposition held
in Buffalo in 1901. The *Buffalo
Courier-Express* described it as
follows: "A Napoleonic wreath in
brilliants, tied with a diamond
ribbon, the ends of which are
represented by two large pearls,
and in the centre of this wreath a
collection of variegated colored
pearls—all of these are unusual
and interesting in the assembly of
precious stones." (October 12, 1901)

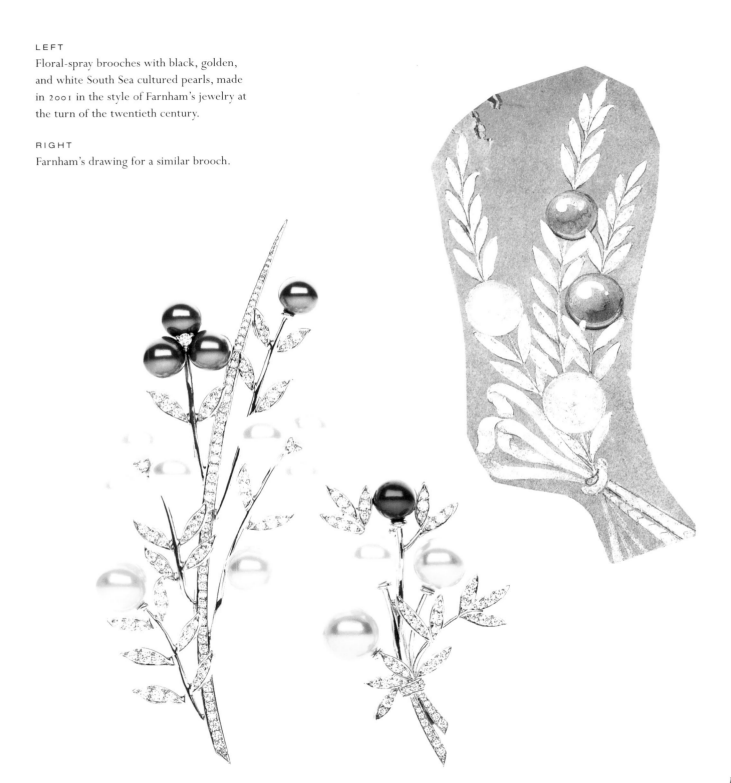

Floral-spray brooches with black, golden,
and white South Sea cultured pearls, made
in 2001 in the style of Farnham's jewelry at
the turn of the twentieth century.

Farnham's drawing for a similar brooch.

shapes, made of natural materials. No longer serious, ceremonial and conspicuous, real jewelry has become accessible and affordable for every secretary and shop girl. It has also become as fashionable—and as faddish—as clothing, and as much an expression of individual taste and mood.

The "simple, softer, sculptural shapes" of pearls were a "natural material" that obviously attracted Elsa Peretti, who in the 1970s and '80s spent several months a year in Japan working with Japan's greatest craftspeople—who lead the world in their respect for nature and its materials. There she discovered the extraordinary beauty of all types of pearls, which the Japanese have such a genius for cultivating: Akoya pearls, mabe pearls, baroque pearls. Her exemplary respect for nature led her to create pendant

OPPOSITE LEFT
Farnham's drawing for a
Renaissance-revival corsage
ornament featuring large
varicolored pearls, intended for
the 1901 Buffalo Exposition.

OPPOSITE RIGHT
Archival photograph of a large
(6¾ by 4¾ inches) corsage
ornament of diamonds and
seven gray pearls shown at the
1901 Buffalo Exposition. It was
priced at $25,000; the pearls
cost a total of $12,059.

RIGHT
Pendant with chased-gold female
figures, four large baroque pearls,
one small baroque pearl, and small
rubies, emeralds, and diamonds.
(Drawing is on page 145, upper
right.)

FOLLOWING SPREAD
Farnham's drawings for
Renaissance-revival brooches with
baroque American pearls, intended
for the 1901 Buffalo Exposition.

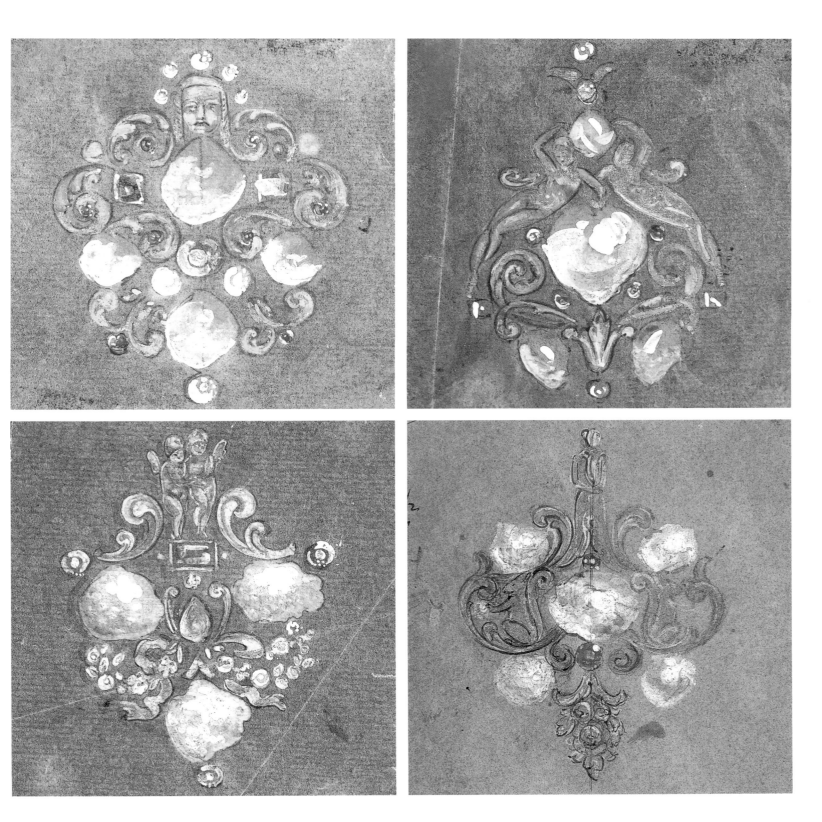

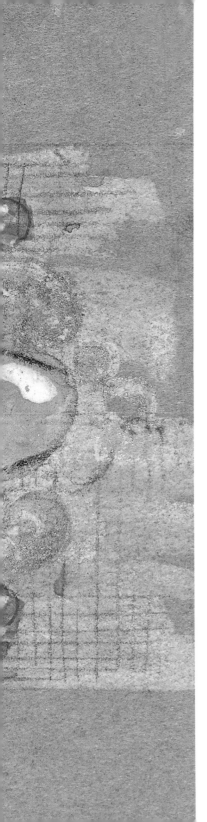

necklaces of large single pearls hung in tasseled nets of black silk so their
natural beauty would not be marred by drilling; and other sculptural pendants of mabe pearls backed with silver, with their irregular surrounds of
nacred shell left untrimmed.

Ferdinando Peretti had noted of his daughter, "She had a wonderful
sense of touch—curiosity in her hands, I call it," and everything in Elsa
Peretti's work is inevitably sensual. It all demands—it shouts out—to be
touched.

She says of her fluid, organic designs: "I love touching soft forms.
Jewelry should complement the wearer, not only visually but also in tac-
tile terms—it should instill a pleasant feeling of desire when worn against
the skin."

And no jewel can compete with the pearl in complementing the wearer
and instilling "a pleasant feeling of desire when worn against the skin."

In October 1980 Pablo Picasso's youngest daughter, Paloma Picasso,
introduced her first Tiffany jewelry collection. Its bold scale and strong
colors at once caught the eyes of both the jewelry and high-fashion worlds.

Her lavish use of colored gemstones soon logically extended to a lavish
use of colored pearls, but unlike Angela Cummings's softly lyrical color
gradations, Picasso's aggressively stylish designs played one color off
another. Soon, there was a memorable, eye-stopping, black-and-white

necklace of one torsade of black pearls looped in front through another torsade of white pearls. Huge colored gemstones caught in diamond pavé ribbons were hung from strands of large baroque South Sea pearls or torsades of Keshi or freshwater Biwa pearls. In an audacious and witty gesture, 15-millimeter mabe pearls were joined two together with domed bands of gold, then strung to create chokers of a more-than-generous scale, even for the 1980s—but of more-than-modest price compared with the so-popular trophy choker of 14-millimeter South Sea pearls. Other mabe pearls were bezel-set in a single row around broad polished cuff bracelets; single large South Sea pearls were perched on gold and diamond X bracelets.

With Elsa Peretti's and Paloma Picasso's brilliantly imaginative and original designs, pearls conquered the territories of high-fashion jewelry that were first so masterfully opened and explored by Jean Schlumberger at Tiffany's fifty years before.

True to its great history with pearls—first led by that eminent pearl authority and champion George Frederick Kunz—Tiffany & Co. today, one hundred and fifty years after Charles Lewis Tiffany's purchase of the famous "Queen Pearl," offers a contemporary collection of pearls gathered from the finest sources throughout the world. From the South Seas to the West Indies, from Japan to the northern Mississippi, from Tahiti to China, they come to Tiffany's—each unique, each "a perfect world enclosed in her sphere" to brighten our lives with their soft, irresistible lunar light.

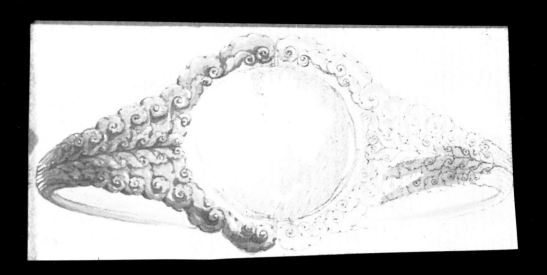

LEFT
Two Farnham proposals
for a gold ring set with an
American baroque pearl.
The notations on the design
below show that it was
approved by Charles T. Cook,
who succeeded Charles L.
Tiffany as president of the
company on March 22, 1902.

OPPOSITE
Circa 1901 drawing for a
gold-and-enamel match
safe depicting a fairy-tale
nocturnal scene illuminated
by a pearl moon.

OPPOSITE
Chrysanthemum brooch of
dogtooth pearls made in 1991
and based on Farnham's 1904
brooch on page 154.

RIGHT
Daisy brooch of diamonds
and American baroque pearls,
circa 1904.

Farnham's chrysanthemum brooch of
dogtooth pearls from the Mississippi
River was made for renowned
operetta star Lillian Russell in 1904.

Chrysanthemum brooch from 1994,
based on Farnham's brooch at left.

LEFT
Portrait of Mary Lily Flagler (1857–1917) wearing a pearl necklace reputed to have cost $2 million. She was the third wife of Henry Morrison Flagler (1830–1913), a partner in Standard Oil who turned his genius to building railroads and developing real estate in Florida. Portrait by Mariette Leslie-Cotton, 1903.

OPPOSITE
Lillian Russell memorabilia. Left: Silver-plated bicycle given to her by her friend "Diamond Jim" Brady. Center: Russell wearing an opera-length pearl necklace. Right: James Brady.

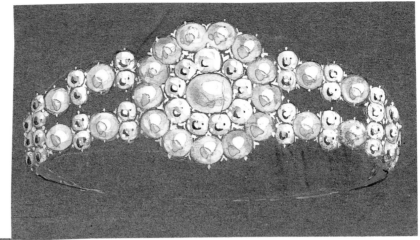

OPPOSITE
Circa 1900 drawing for a pearl
necklace with diamond bows.

RIGHT
Circa 1900 drawings for pearl
chokers that could be worn as
bracelets by adjusting their
closures.

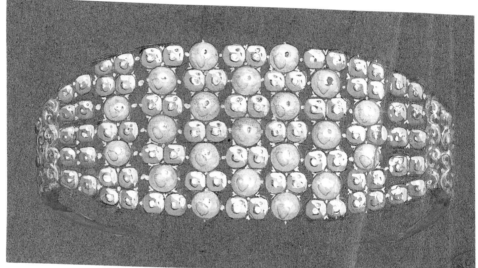

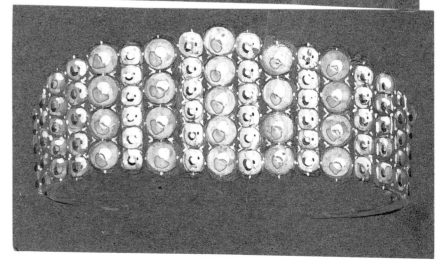

159

ABOVE
"Lacings" seed-pearl and diamond
choker, designed in 1994 in the
style of 1900.

OPPOSITE
"Buckle" necklace and bracelet
designed in 1997 in the style
of 1900.

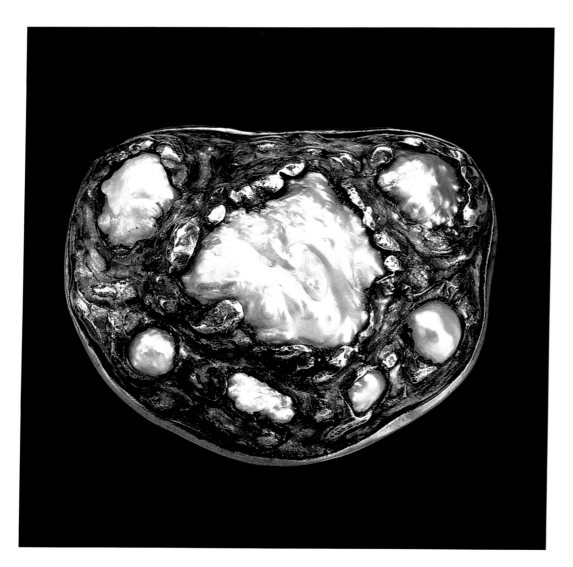

Louis Comfort Tiffany's circa
1906 gold and enamel-on-silver
seaweed-motif brooch, set with
American baroque freshwater
pearls. *Louis Comfort Tiffany
Garden Museum, Matsue, Japan*

Enameled seaweed-motif brooch
with a large central pearl and
three smaller pearls, designed by
Louis Comfort Tiffany, circa 1906.

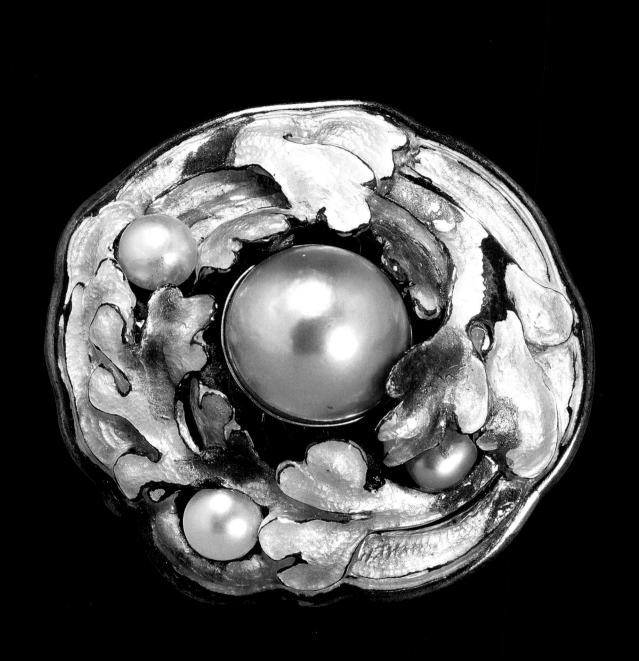

Circa 1906 Etruscan-style bib necklace designed by Louis Comfort Tiffany. Round filigree elements with seed pearls alternate with round elements with filigree loops. The collar has small baroque-pearl links, and the drops are dogtooth pearls. Signed "Louis C. Tiffany, Artist." *Louis Comfort Tiffany Garden Museum, Matsue, Japan*

RIGHT

Necklace with a pendant centered
by a kunzite, with baroque pearls,
amethysts, and demantoids. The
double chain is set with baroque
pearls, demantoids, and Montana
sapphires. Made circa 1918 under the
direction of Louis Comfort Tiffany.

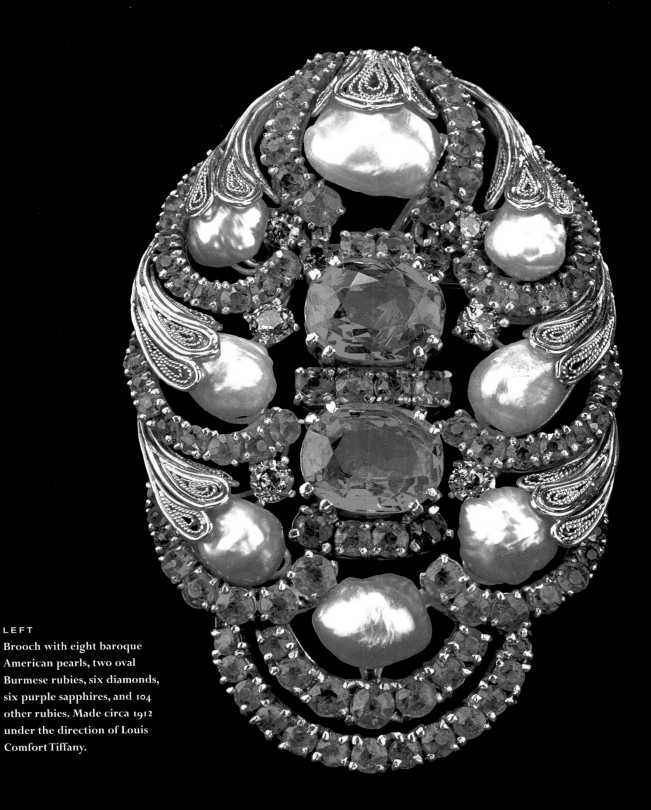

Conch-pearl and diamond
necklace, circa 1910.

RIGHT
Conch-pearl and diamond
necklace featured in *Vogue's*
February 2004 issue. Photograph by Raymond Meier.

Diamond, tsavorite, and pink
tourmaline brooches centered
with cultured Tahitian pearls. Made
in 2005, they were inspired by the
circa 1920 brooch on page 174.

TIFFANY & CO.
FIFTH AVENUE & 37ᵀᴴ STREET

ROPES OF PEARLS

Form 3122A lines D.C., 1921.

New York Daily Papers.

OPPOSITE
Center: Tiffany's ran this
newspaper advertisement
countless times in the 1920s.

RIGHT
Russell Ball's 1928 photograph
of Paramount Pictures star
Esther Ralston (1902–1994)
wearing ropes of imitation
pearls. Like the pearls Audrey
Hepburn wore in *Breakfast at
Tiffany's* thirty-three years later,
they came from Paramount's
costume department.

OPPOSITE
Diamond-and-platinum circle
brooch centered with a large
gray pearl, circa 1920.

RIGHT
"Jazz" 1920s art deco–style
diamond pendant and earrings
with cultured South Sea pearl
drops made in 2004.

LEFT
Diamond-and-platinum ring with
a cultured South Sea pearl, made
in 2004 in the 1920s art deco
style.

OPPOSITE
Foreground: Pearl-and-diamond
bracelet, circa 1920. Background:
Drawings for an emerald-and-
diamond bracelet and a cabochon-
sapphire-and-diamond brooch of
the same period.

LEFT
De Molas's photograph from
Vogue's issue dated May 1, 1939,
featured dresses and hats from
Henri Bendel and jewelry from
Tiffany's. The model at left wears
a pearl necklace and a clip with a
large gray pearl surrounded by
diamonds. The model at right
wears a double-strand pearl
necklace.

OPPOSITE
Cultured-pearl pendants on
diamond-studded chains, made
in 2005 in the style of the
1920s. Left: South Sea pearls.
Right: Tahitian black pearl.

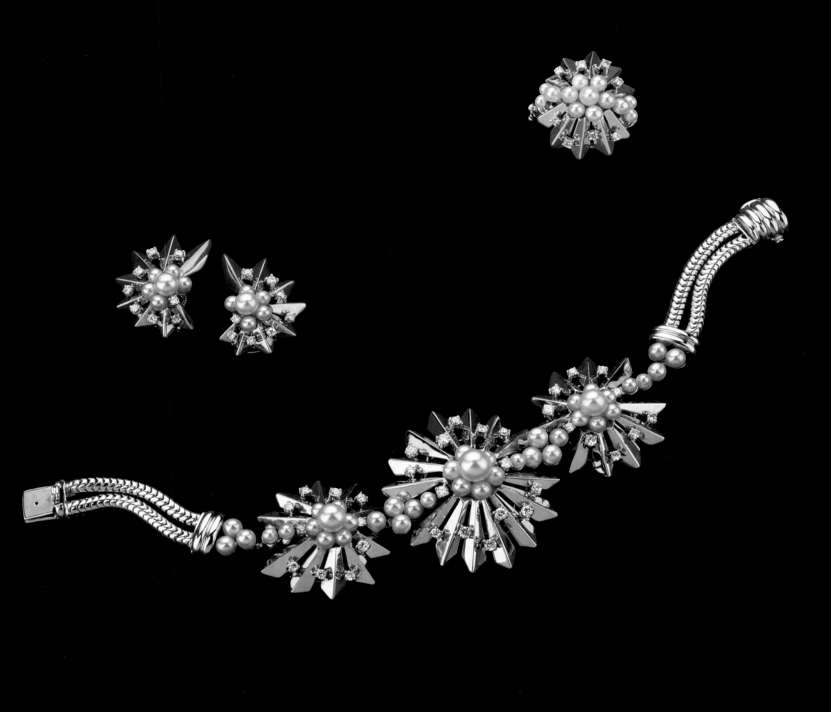

OPPOSITE
Eric Carl Ericson's fashion
illustration from *Vogue* issue
dated July 1, 1933, shows
models wearing (left) a pearl
necklace and a "Tiffany blue"
crépe evening dress by Molyneux
and (right), a yellow flannel
jacket over a flowered crépe
evening dress by Patou.

BELOW
Tiffany's advertisement in
Harper's Bazaar's December 1935
issue offered "Pearl Necklaces
$200 to $470,000." The two
pearl necklaces illustrated were
priced at $425 and $3,850.

A page from Tiffany's 1950 catalog. The double-strand natural-pearl necklace was priced at $19,800, and the brooch with the famous 75-carat emerald formerly owned by Turkish sultan Abdul Hamid (and now in the Smithsonian Institution's Hall of Gems) was priced at $39,000, only twice the price of the necklace.

A page from Tiffany's 1951 catalog again indicates the high prices for natural pearls relative to other gems. The necklace of sixty-seven graduated pearls was priced at $31,800; the 15½-inch necklace of fifty-one diamonds totaling 24 carats was priced at $19,500.

Publicity photographs for *Breakfast at Tiffany's* (1961) showing Audrey Hepburn wearing a four-strand pearl necklace, which, like Esther Ralston's ropes of pearls (see page 173), were imitations from Paramount's costume department.

Jean Schlumberger's "Wings" clip of cultured baroque pearls and diamond clusters in 18-karat gold. Schlumberger (1907–1987) began designing jewelry for Paris couturière Elsa Schiaparelli in 1936, opened his first New York shop in 1947, and joined Tiffany & Co. in 1956, the year he designed this clip.

Elizabeth Taylor's bare back displaying a four-strand Tiffany cultured-pearl necklace, in Richard Avedon's photograph for the September 1960 issue of *Harper's Bazaar,* which described the necklace as "a cape of pearls—epic in size, incredible in their creamy rose luster."

Multistrand necklaces of white seed pearls, golden seed pearls, and coral beads, photographed by James Moore for *Harper's Bazaar,* April 1967.

RIGHT

Cultured-pearl necklace centered by a pear-shaped tanzanite surrounded by diamonds, and matching earclips. Photographed by Jerry Salvati for *Town & Country*, December 1969.

LEFT
Charlene Dash modeling Jean Schlumberger's "Sheaves of Wheat" necklace of seed pearls, lapis lazuli beads, yellow and white diamonds, and sapphires set in platinum and 18-karat gold. Gianni Penati's photograph for *Vogue,* September 15, 1970.

OPPOSITE
Cultured-pearl necklace with diamond flowers and buds, designed in 1971 by Jean Schlumberger for philanthropist Margaret L. Burden (1910–1996).

Schlumberger's dog collar of cultured
pearls, lapis lazuli, and diamonds,
designed in 1971.

Schlumberger's diamond-pavé and
pailloné-enamel "Wings" clip with a
pendant pear-shaped cultured Tahitian
pearl, originally designed in 1968.

Françoise de la Renta (1921–1983), wife of fashion designer Oscar de la Renta and editor-at-large at *Vogue*. She wears Schlumberger's seed-pearl necklace with paillonè enamel clasps. Both she and Jean Schlumberger began their careers working for Elsa Schiaparelli. Photographed by Eric Boman for the *New York Times Magazine*, December 21, 1980.

OPPOSITE
Schlumberger's "Buckle" necklace of cultured South Sea pearls.

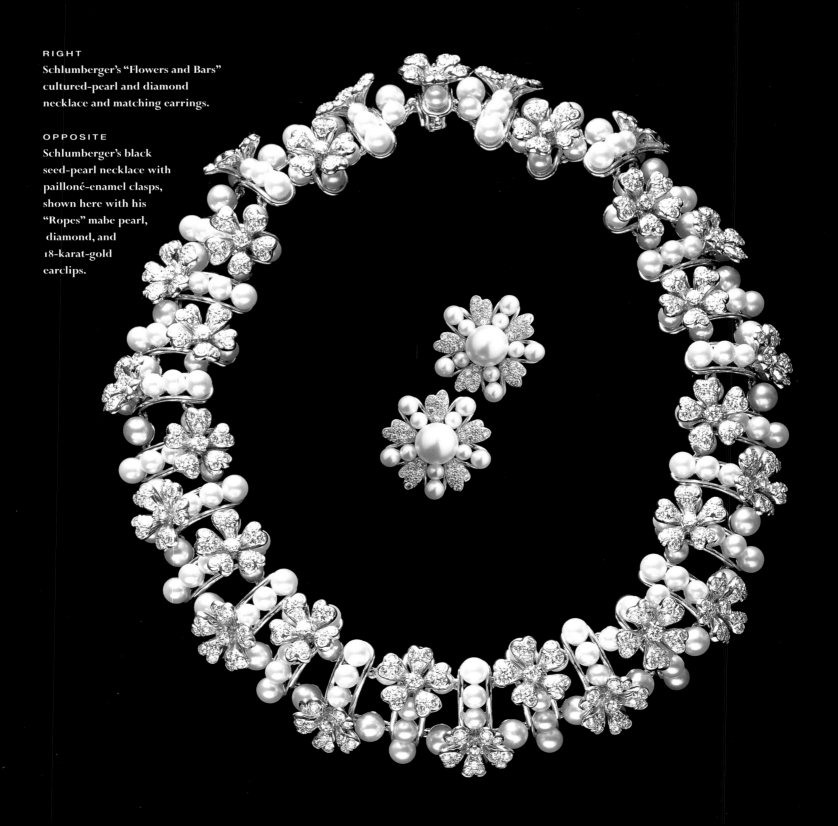

RIGHT
Schlumberger's "Flowers and Bars"
cultured-pearl and diamond
necklace and matching earrings.

OPPOSITE
Schlumberger's black
seed-pearl necklace with
pailloné-enamel clasps,
shown here with his
"Ropes" mabe pearl,
 diamond, and
18-karat-gold
earclips.

LEFT
Schlumberger's 33-inch "Pebbles and Beans" necklace of cultured pearls and pavé diamonds.

BELOW
Schlumberger's cultured baroque pearl and diamond earclips.

205

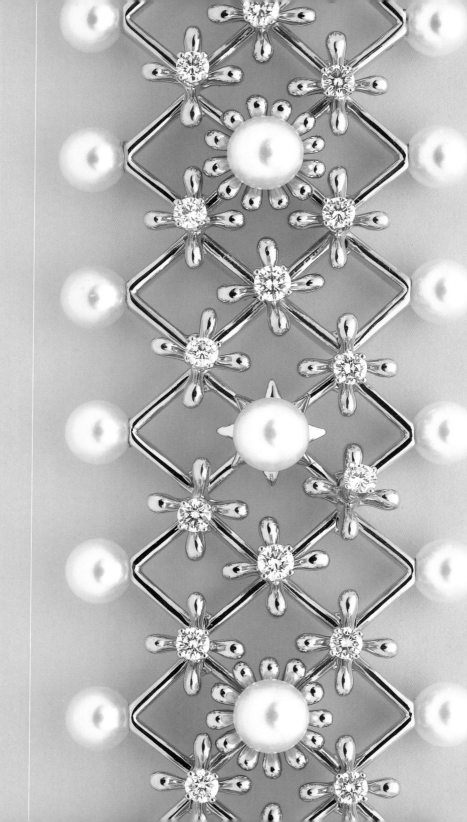

OPPOSITE
Schlumberger's "Flowers and
Stars" bracelet.

THIS PAGE
Schlumberger's "Sea Flower" clip.

OPPOSITE
Eleven-strand cultured-pearl choker,
ring with a cultured baroque pearl,
and earclips with cultured baroque
pearls surrounded by tiny diamonds,
designed by Angela Cummings in 1980.

LEFT
Seed-pearl lariat designed by Angela
Cummings in 1980.

Forty-seven-inch-long gold "lariat" with ten cultured Biwa pearls, designed by Angela Cummings in 1978. She designed jewelry for Tiffany's from 1968 to 1984.

Five-strand cultured-pearl necklace with a diamond-swirl center and matching diamond-swirl earclips. Designed by Angela Cummings in 1980.

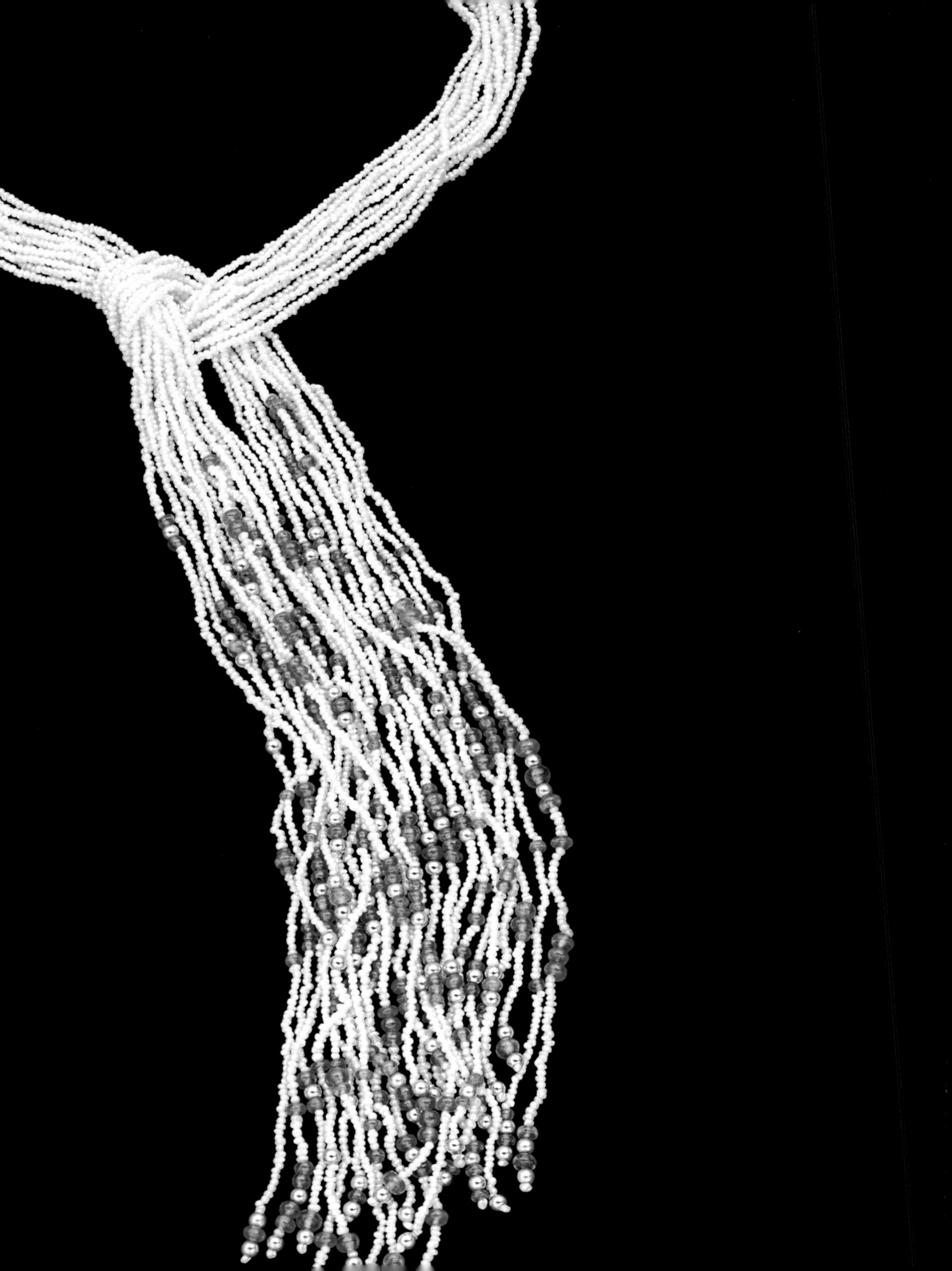

RIGHT
Lariat of seed pearls with ruby and gold beads, designed by Angela Cummings in 1981.

OPPOSITE
Necklace of cultured lavender freshwater pearls fronted by a diamond-pavé egg-shape ornament studded with cabochon rubies, designed by Angela Cummings in 1981.

Stan Malinowski's photograph
for *Vogue's* 1980 Christmas issue
shows Kelly LeBrock modeling
a wide array of cultured-pearl
jewelry designed by Angela
Cummings. The necklace at far
left is strung with keshi pearls
from Tahiti; the lariat around her
neck and draped over her arm
is strung with freshwater "Rice
Krispie" baroque pearls cultured
in China from cockscomb
mussels; the clasp of the bracelet
is set with a large baroque pearl.

RIGHT
Odile Broulard modeling a
multistrand cultured-pearl
necklace with a diamond
ribbon cross centered by a
large cultured Burmese pearl,
with matching earclips and
ring. Photographed by Victor
Skrebneski for *Town & Country's*
February 1990 issue.

A spread of cultured-pearl jewelry from Tiffany's 1984–1985 catalog. At center is a necklace of thirty-three pearls graduated from 10.7 millimeters to 14.4 millimeters. Upper left: "Star" earclips with mabe pearls; upper center: "Wing" earclips; lower left: "Starfish" earclips; upper right: White Burmese pearl and black Tahitian pearl clips with detachable drops; center right: Pearl earclips; lower right: Earclips with South Sea mabe pearls.

Elsa Peretti wearing her cultured-pearl earrings in her garden overlooking Porto Ercole. A former design student and fashion model, Elsa Peretti became one of Tiffany's leading jewelry designers in 1974. Photographed by François Halard for *House & Garden,* October 1988.

Gold mesh necklace with a cultured-pearl fringe, designed by Elsa Peretti in 2000. Original design © Elsa Peretti.

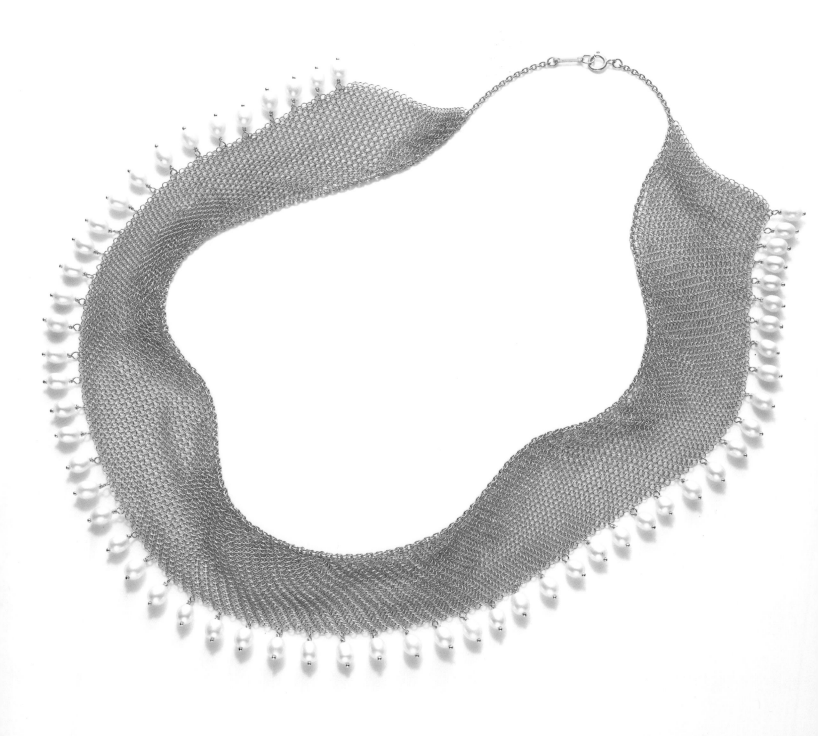

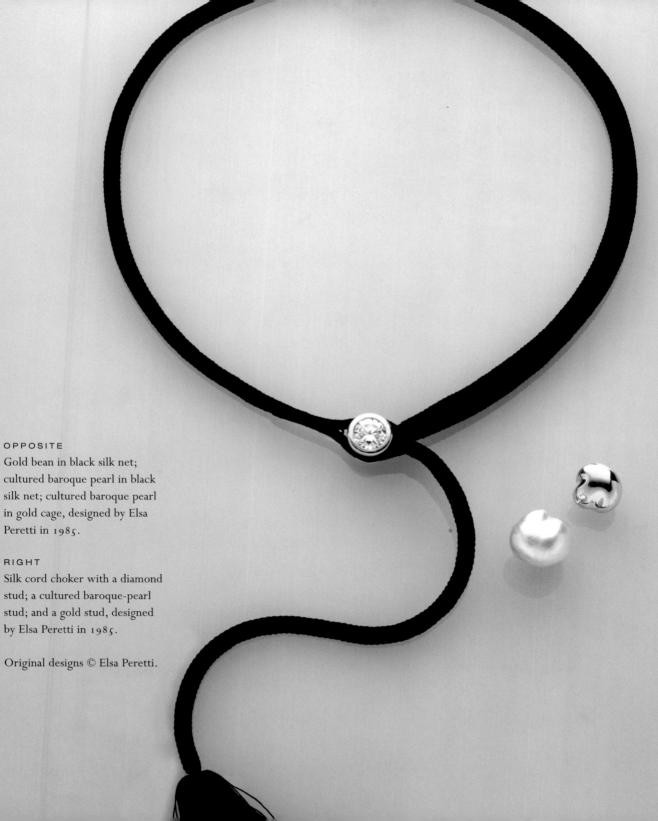

OPPOSITE
Gold bean in black silk net;
cultured baroque pearl in black
silk net; cultured baroque pearl
in gold cage, designed by Elsa
Peretti in 1985.

RIGHT
Silk cord choker with a diamond
stud; a cultured baroque-pearl
stud; and a gold stud, designed
by Elsa Peretti in 1985.

Original designs © Elsa Peretti.

ABOVE
Elsa Peretti's platinum charm
bracelet with a cultured baroque
black pearl, 1999.

OPPOSITE
Elsa Peretti's 18-karat gold
flexible snake necklace and
"Bird Head" cultured baroque-
pearl brooch, designed in 1985.

Original designs © Elsa Peretti.

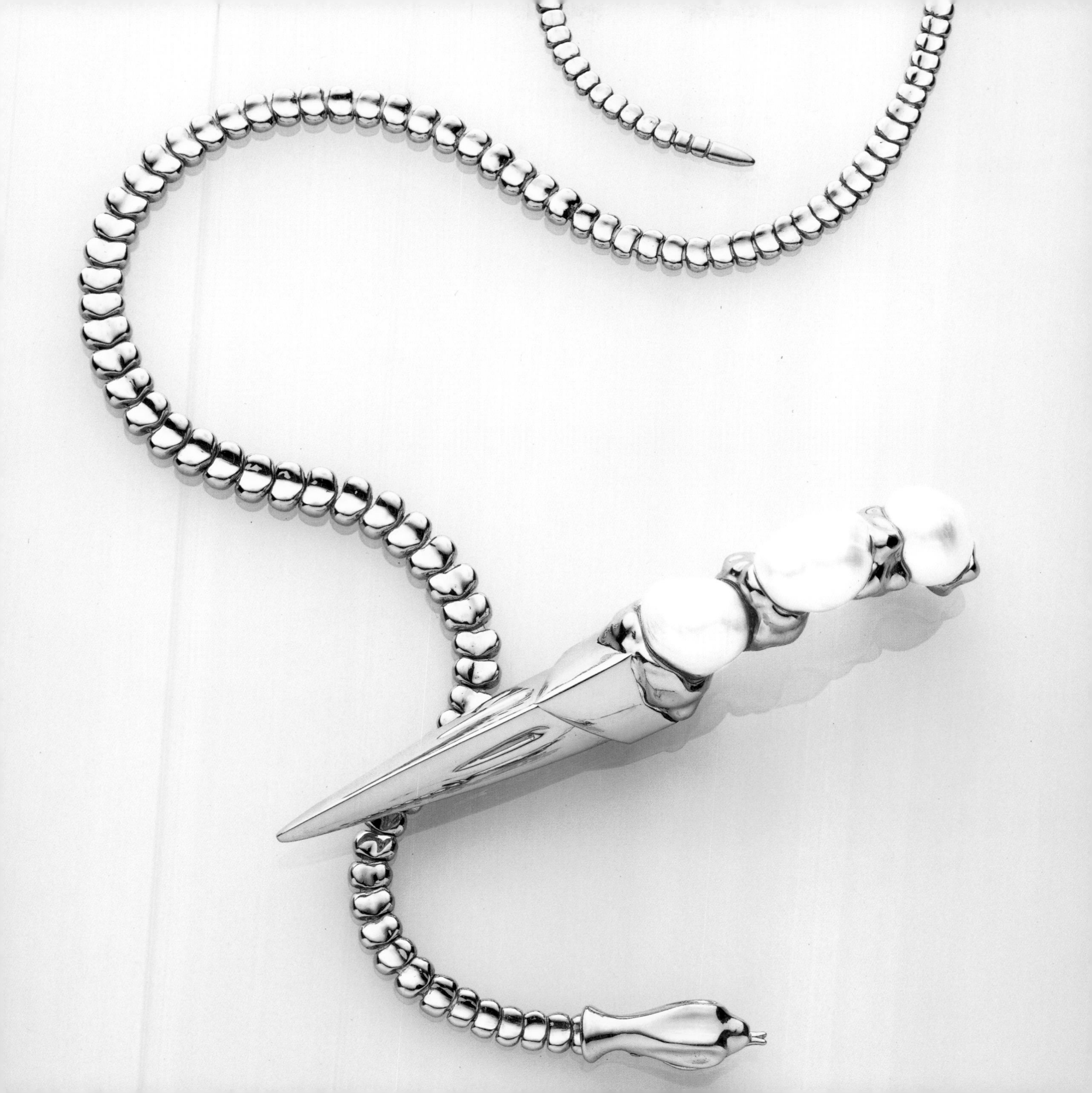

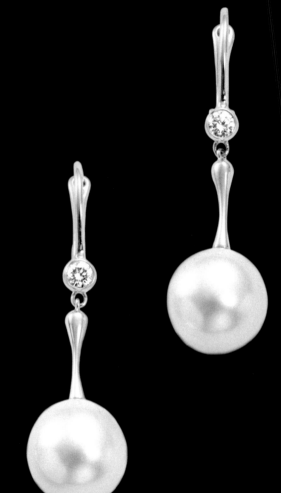

OPPOSITE
Elsa Peretti's diamond ear studs with
detachable cultured-pearl drops and
her cultured-pearl drop earrings.

RIGHT
Christy Turlington modeling
Peretti's cultured-pearl drop earrings
(opposite right) and a minidress
by Lisa Bruce, photographed by
Francesco Scavullo for the cover
of *Cosmopolitan*, June 1993.

Original designs © Elsa Peretti.

227

Elsa Peretti's "Diamonds-by-the-Yard" with
Tahitian cultured keshi pearls and rubies,
2001. Original design © Elsa Peretti.

Paloma Picasso's black and white cultured-pearl necklace with an 18-karat gold clasp, 1981. The daughter of Pablo Picasso and Françoise Gilot, Paloma designed her first jewelry collection for Tiffany's in 1980. Original design © Paloma Picasso.

233

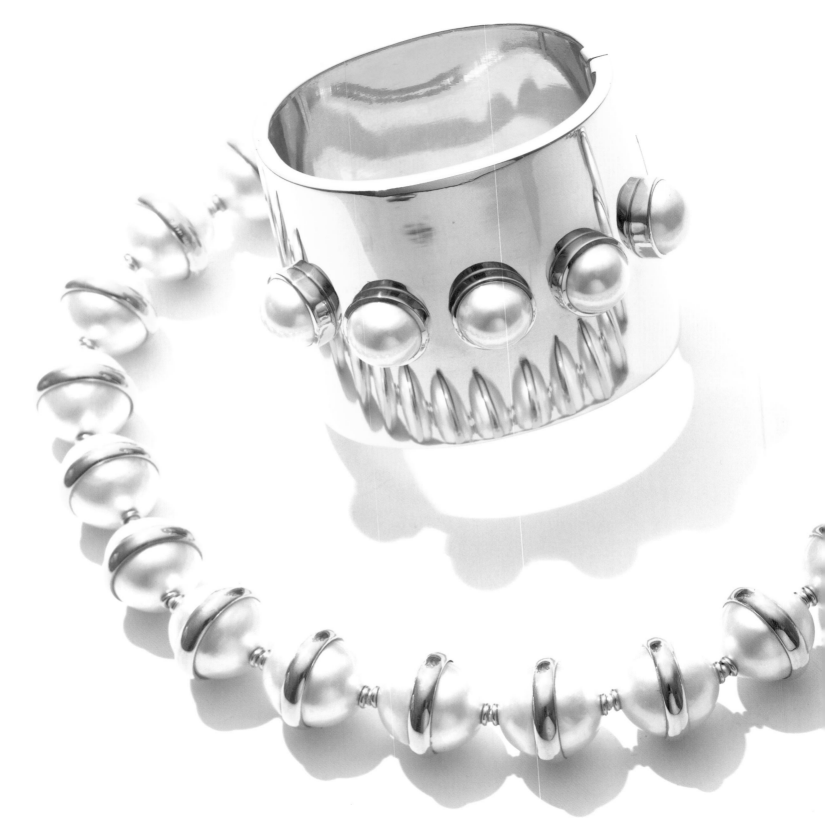

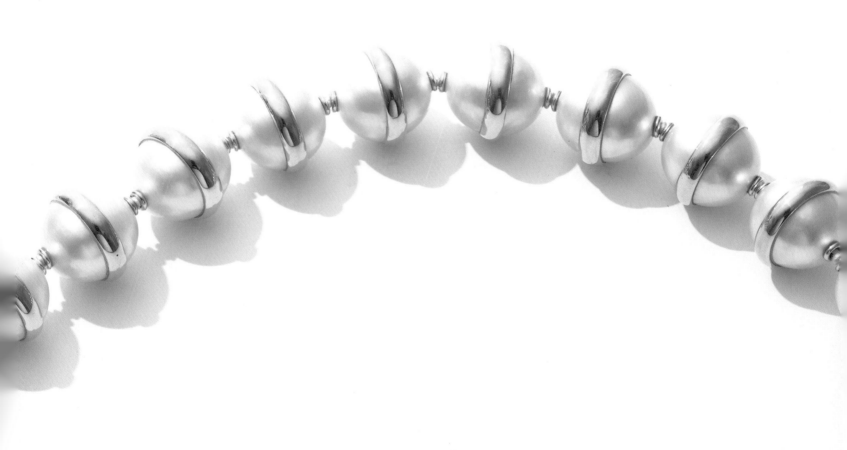

Paloma Picasso's cuff bracelet of
18-karat gold and mabe pearls, and
her necklace of mabe pearls, 1989.
Original designs © Paloma Picasso.

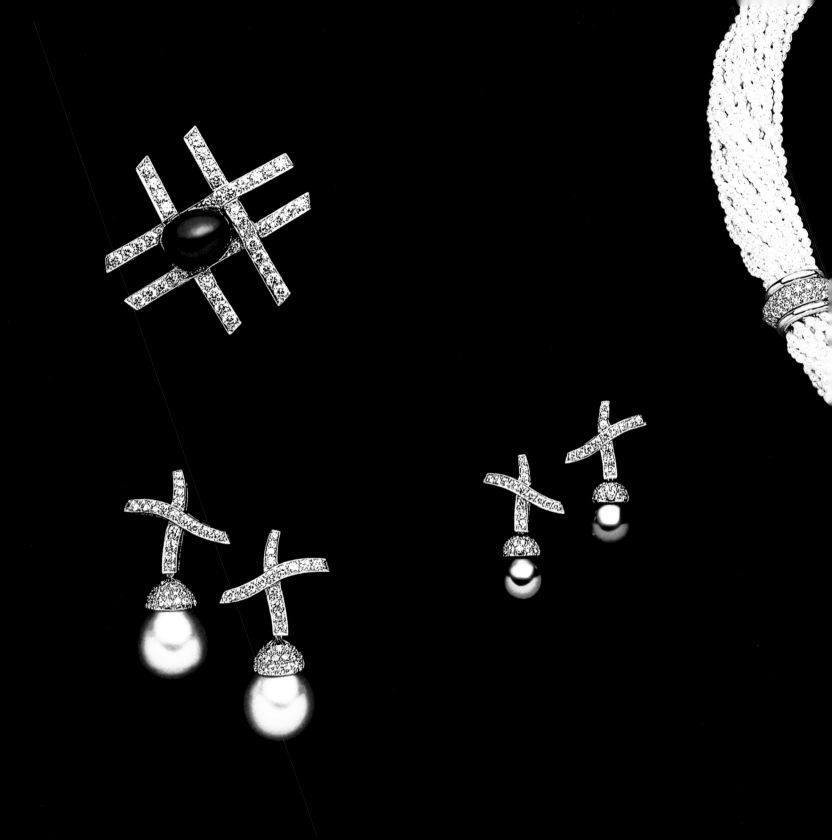

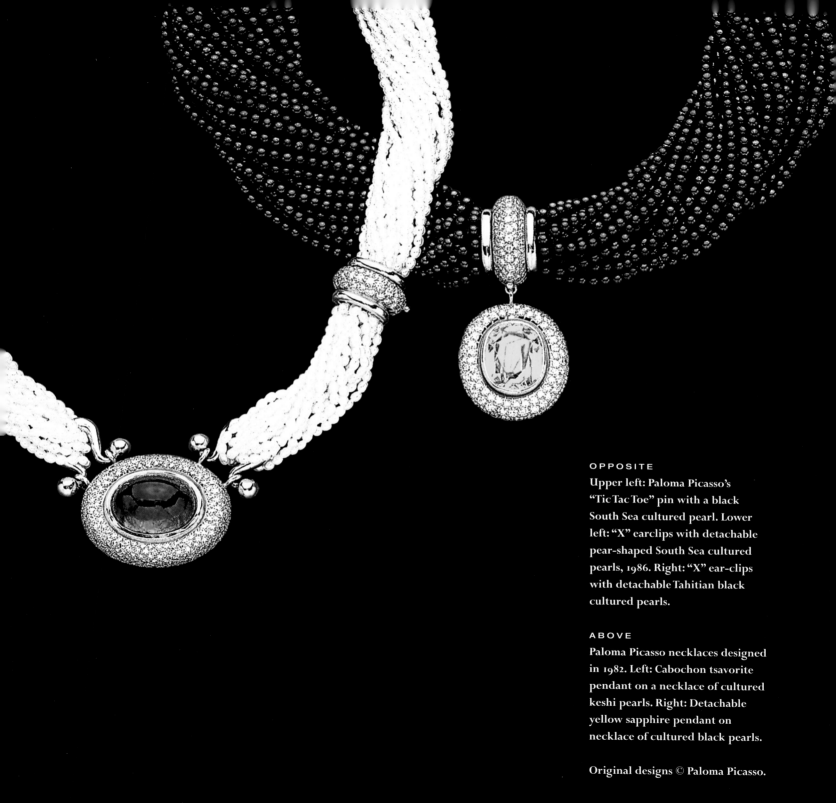

THIS PAGE
Paloma Picasso's "X" bangle
bracelets centered by cultured
South Sea pearls, 1986.

OPPOSITE
Picasso holding her multistrand
cultured-pearl necklace with a large
briolette amethyst pendant and
wearing her polygonal amethyst ring
and aquamarine briolette earrings.

Original designs © Paloma Picasso.

OPPOSITE
Andrea modeling a thirty-inch strand of
cultured South Sea pearls with matching
earrings at a 1989 show for the fashion
press at Tiffany's New York store.

BELOW
Silver earclips with cultured pearls
and amethysts and matching brooch
with cultured pearls, 1989.

RIGHT
Enamel and diamond-pavé
floral brooch with golden,
black, and white cultured
South Sea pearls, 2000.

OPPOSITE
"Fireworks" brooches with
South Sea cultured pearls,
yellow and white diamonds, and
pink and green tourmalines.

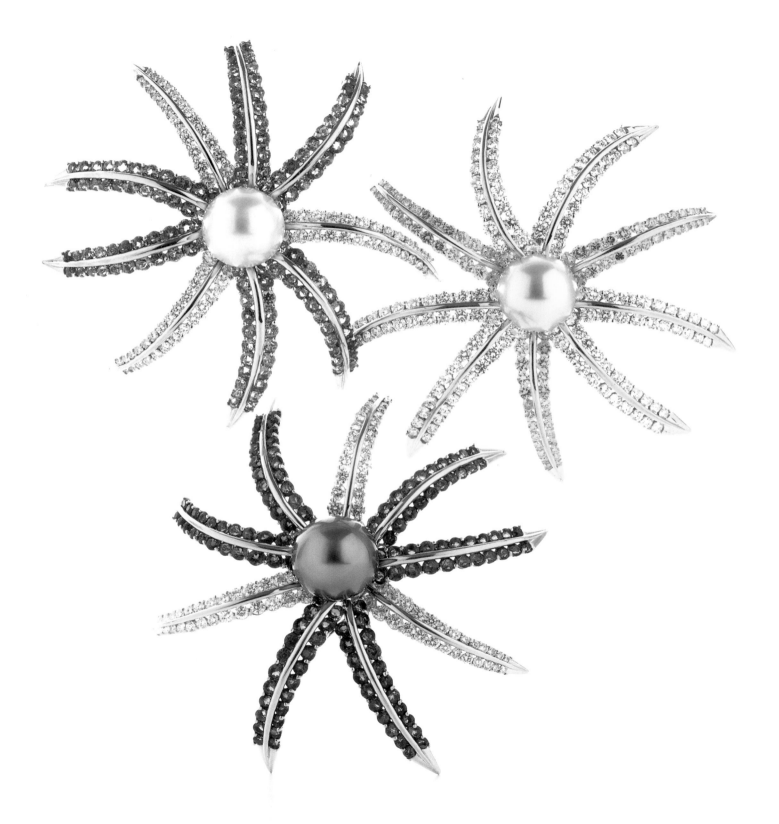

BELOW

Double-strand cultured white-
pearl necklace with a detachable
cultured black pearl and
diamond "Fireworks" brooch.

OPPOSITE

"Fireworks" cuff bracelet with
South Sea cultured pearls.

OPPOSITE
Heather Stewart Whyte
modeling a classic cultured-
pearl necklace and earrings,
1994.

RIGHT
Isabella Scorupca modeling
a Tahitian cultured-pearl
necklace, 1994.

OPPOSITE
"Tiffany Lace" diamond necklace
and earrings with cultured keshi
pearl drops.

THIS PAGE
Left: Neck chains with white and
black cultured South Sea pearl
pendants, 1995. Right: Drop
earrings with black and white
cultured pearls, 1995.

BELOW

"Tiffany Nature" cultured-pearl jewelry inspired by Stanford White's oyster crab necklace.

OPPOSITE

Oyster crab gold-and-pearl necklace designed by the great architect Stanford White and made by Tiffany's for his bride, Bessie Springs Smith, for their wedding on February 7, 1884.

OPPOSITE
The necklace (this page) photographed
in the style of Gene Moore's Tiffany
window displays.

RIGHT
South Sea cultured pearl and diamond-
pavé link necklace and earrings, 1998.

257

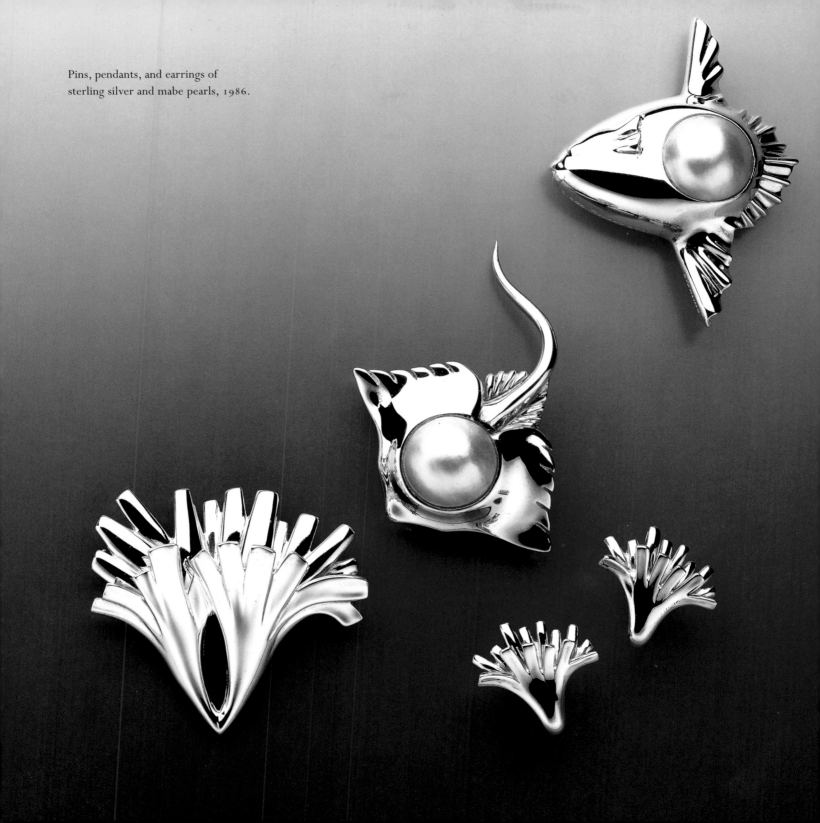

Pins, pendants, and earrings of
sterling silver and mabe pearls, 1986.

BELOW

"Tiffany Nature" cultured-pearl bracelet with a sterling silver dragonfly, 1998.

OPPOSITE

"Tiffany Nature" daimond-pavé frog pins, two with South Sea and Tahitian cultured pearls, 1996.

THIS PAGE
Three-strand "Breakaway" necklace of
Tahitian cultured pearls with diamond-
pavé spacers, 1997.

OPPOSITE
Triple-strand necklace of cultured white,
Tahitian, and golden pearls, 1998.

Double-strand necklace of cultured
Akoya pearls with diamond-pavé-and-ruby
ornaments and matching earrings, 1998.

ABOVE
Model wearing the triple-strand
necklace shown at right.

RIGHT
Triple-strand necklace of cultured
South Sea pearls with diamond-pavé
orchid clasp, 2001.

"Fish" brooch and earrings with
tsavorites, blue and pink sapphires,
diamonds, rubies, and South Sea
cultured pearls, designed in 1993.

"Twin Fish" brooch of sapphires,
tsavorites, diamonds, black onyx, and
a South Sea cultured pearl, 2004.

RIGHT

ER star Michael Michelle wearing
Karl Lagerfeld's 1990 version of
Coco Chanel's 1920s classic crêpe
"little black dress," a Tahitian
and South Sea cultured-pearl
bracelet with diamond spacers,
and diamond earrings.

OPPOSITE

Michael Michelle wearing
a satin cocktail dress by Karl
Lagerfeld for Chanel, diamond
earrings with cultured Tahitian
pearl drops, and double-strand
cultured-pearl bracelets. Both
photographs by Gerald Foster for
Town & Country, January 2003.

OPPOSITE
Necklace of cultured keshi
pearls and diamonds, 2001.

THIS PAGE
Sarah Jessica Parker wearing
the "Wave" necklace along with
matching earrings. Photograph
by Eric Boman.

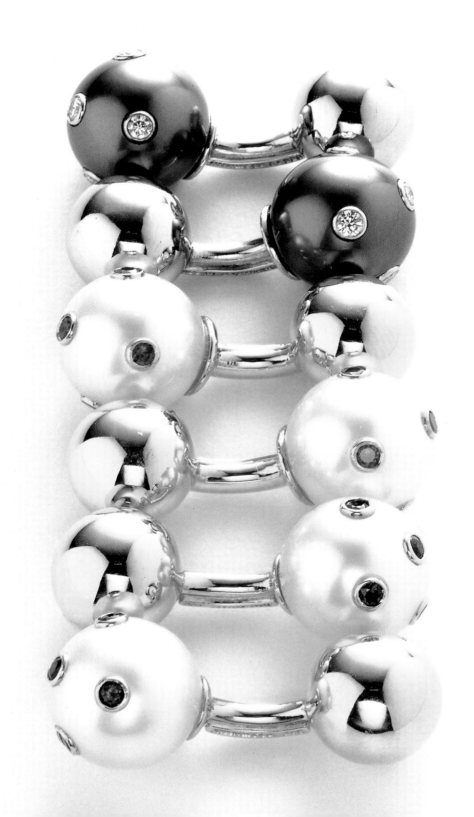

OPPOSITE
"Étoile" cuff links of gold,
platinum, and cultured South Sea
pearls studded with diamonds,
rubies, and sapphires, 2001.

BELOW
Necklace of cultured Tahitian,
white, and golden pearls with
diamond spacers, 2001.

THIS PAGE

"Petal" cultured golden South Sea
pearl and diamond-pavé necklace
with matching earrings, 1998.

OPPOSITE

"Tiffany Rose" diamond necklace
with cultured golden South Sea
pearl drops, 2004.

Brooches of diamond-pavé coral
branches set with conch pearls, 2004.

"Tiffany Voile" earrings with conch
pearl drops, 2004.

Diamond pendant with a whopping
172-grain conch pearl (the largest
reported gem-quality conch pearl
weighed 180 grains); the pendant
is based on the Walters Museum
pendant shown on page 119.

Cultured Tahitian pearl
pendants on platinum chains
with diamonds, tsavorites,
pink tourmalines, and
moonstones, 2005.

THIS PAGE
South Sea varicolored cultured-pearl necklace with diamond-pavé buckle clasp, 2005.

OPPOSITE
South Sea varicolored cultured-pearl necklace with diamond-pavé sphere, 2005.

OPPOSITE
Valentina Zelyaeva modeling
a diamond necklace with
South Sea cultured-pearl
pendants and a Gucci jacket.
Photograph by Sølve Sundsbø
for the cover of *Harper's
Bazaar*, October 2004.

RIGHT
International opera diva
Renée Fleming wearing a
South Sea cultured-pearl
necklace with a diamond-
pavé trefoil clasp.
Photograph by Matthew
Rolston for *Town & Country*,
January 2005.

OPPOSITE
Necklace of large cultured
Tahitian pearls with a flowerlike
clasp of pear-shaped and round
brilliant-cut diamonds, 2005.

RIGHT
Cultured South Sea pearl necklace
with diamond-pavé sphere, 2005.

RIGHT

Model Shalom Harlow wearing a cultured South Sea pearl necklace. Her escort wears cultured-pearl studs and cuff links.

Abalone pearls
Abalones are marine gastropods found on rocky shores throughout much of the world. Their pearls have a bluish or greenish tint with flashes of pink and lavender.

Akoya pearls
Pinctada fucata oysters once flourished naturally in Japan's Ago Bay. In the early twentieth century, Kokichi Mikimoto (1858–1954) and other pioneers developed modern perliculture using Akoya pearl oysters; they remain extensively cultured today.

Baroque
Term for irregular pearls. The French word *baroque* (curious, odd, or strange) was applied to irregular pearls before it was used—initially in a derogatory sense—for painting, sculpture, and architecture of the seventeenth century.

Baler shell
The marine gastropod *Melo melo* is found in the South China Sea and off Singapore and Malaysia. Its orange-tinted, non-nacreous melo pearls (which cannot be cultured) are highly prized.

Biwa pearls
Cultured freshwater pearls from Biwa pearl mussels, *Hyriopsis schegelii,* native to Lake Biwa in Japan and now grown in lakes and streams in the vicinity.

Black pearls
Many so-called "black" pearls are brown or gray; their iridescence is often tinted with green, blue, or rose.

Blister pearls
Pearls formed in the nacreous surface inside the shell.

Burmese pearls
Pearls from the South Sea silver-lipped or golden-lipped pearl oyster, *Pinctada maxima,* traditionally fished by Malay-speaking maritime nomads called the Mawken in the three thousand–island Mergui Archipelago off the southern coast of Burma. In the late nineteenth century, Burmese pearl fishing expanded rapidly, leading to overharvesting in the early twentieth century. Perliculture was introduced in 1954 and expanded in the 1960s; Tiffany's introduced Burmese cultured pearls in 1964. They can be as large as 18 millimeters and are noted for their luster. (Burma was renamed Myanmar in 1989.)

Chinese pearls
Although freshwater blister pearls were cultured in China as early as 5000 BC, modern Chinese perliculture dates from the 1960s. It began with small, irregular, inexpensive "Rice Krispie" pearls cultured from cockscomb mussels, *Cristaria plicata*. In the 1980s Chinese pearl farms began culturing pearls from triangleshell mussels, *Hyriopsis cumingii*. China's production from triangleshells now includes gem-quality round pearls rivaling Akoya, South Sea, and Tahitian pearls.

Conch pearls
Produced by the queen conch, *Strombus gigas,* a marine gastropod found in the Florida Keys and the Bahamas, conch pearls are non-nacreous but have a silky, flamelike, or moiré luster called *chatoyancy*. Most often pink, their colors can range from white to yellow, beige, and lavender. Attempts at culturing conch pearls have so far been unsuccessful: all conch pearls in the gem market are natural.

Cultured pearls
Modern perliculture was developed in Japan in the early twentieth century. It involves inserting a bead nucleus with a piece of mantle (the tissue that creates the nacreous surface inside the shell and can create pearls). This technique was developed in part by Kokochi Mikimoto, who originated the term *cultured pearls* and promoted them with great success. When sales of natural pearls fell during the Great Depression, a European pearl syndicate sued Mikimoto, alleging that his pearls were "fakes." Mikimoto's defense included scientific testimony asserting that cultured pearls had

exactly the same substance and color as natural pearls, the only difference being that their nuclei were artificially introduced, and Mikimoto won the lawsuit. Even so, the most prestigious jewelry companies—including Tiffany's—declined to offer cultured pearls to the public until the 1950s. Since then the gem pearl trade has been entirely dominated by cultured pearls, and fishing for natural pearls has nearly ceased. Tiffany's continues to use the term *cultured pearls*.

Demantoids
Rare green garnets from the Ural Mountains in Russia.

Dogtooth pearls
Elongated baroque pearls from washboard pearl mussels, *Megalonaias nervosa,* found in the Mississippi River and its tributaries.

Free pearls
Pearls that are not attached to the interior of the shell, i.e., not blister pearls.

Half pearls
Blister pearls or mabe pearls.

Keshi pearls
The term was formerly used for small (1–2 millimeter) "chance" pearls inadvertently resulting from cultured pearl nucleation. Today the term is used for larger chance pearls (up to 10 millimeters) produced without nucleation in cultured-pearl fisheries; although keshi pearls result from human intervention, there is no physical difference between keshi pearls and natural pearls. They often show a high degree of orient.

La Paz pearls
Black pearls from La Paz in Baja California were highly prized in the late nineteenth century, but the pearl beds were almost totally depleted by 1900. A century later they were revived for culturing mabe pearls and then round pearls; an estimated 1,500 pearls from La Paz pearl oysters, *Pinctada mazatlantica,* were cultured in 1999.

Mabe pearls
Hemispherical blister pearls cultured by inserting a dome-shaped mold inside the shell under the mantle. Kokichi Mikimoto originated mabe pearls circa 1896 by culturing *Pteria penguin.* They are now cultured from other bivalves and abalones. Mabe pearls of equal size are sometimes joined together with a band (usually gold) to simulate a round pearl.

Melo pearls
See baler shell.

Nacre
Lustrous material secreted in layers to form pearls and mother-of-pearl.

Nucleation
Human insertion of spherical beads into a mollusk to induce formation of cultured pearls. For many years most beads were made from the shells of pigtoe mussels, *Pleurobema cordatum,* from the Tennessee River. Due to overfishing and pollution, pigtoes are now protected, and shells from about ten other species found in Tennessee and Alabama are used instead; about half the beads are made from the shells of washboard mussels, *Megalonaias nervosa*.

Orient
Term for a pearl's iridescence or rainbowlike effect. It is most evident in baroque pearls with "pools" of nacre.

Oriental pearls
Natural pearls from the Persian Gulf and the Gulf of Mannar between India and Ceylon, the sources of 75 percent of the world's gem-quality pearl production in the early twentieth century. The term was formerly used to distinguish such pearls from freshwater pearls, American pearls, and cultured pearls.

Pearls

Most nacreous gem-quality pearls are produced by relatively few species of bivalve mollusks, primarily marine oysters and freshwater mussels. Non-nacreous gem-quality pearls are produced by queen conches and baler shells.

Round

Jewelers' term for spherical pearls.

Seed pearls

Pearls smaller than 2 millimeters in diameter or 0.25 grains. Popular in the mid-nineteenth century, when most seed pearls were fished in the waters off Ceylon and strung on white horsehairs in China.

Size

In the past pearls were sized by their weight in grains and occasionally in carats. Today, in part because most cultured pearls are round, they are usually sized by their diameter in millimeters. George Frederick Kunz used scales and calipers to develop a table of equivalents that he called the "Kunz gage," a portion of which is shown below. Round natural pearls larger than 14 grains (8 millimeters) are rare.

Grains	Diam. in Millimeters
¼	2.1
½	2.7
1	3.3
2	4.2
5	5.7
10	7.2
15	8.2
30	10.3
60	13.0
100	15.4
200	19.4
400	24.5

South Sea pearls

Cultured from the Silver- or Gold-lipped pearl oyster, *Pinctada maxima,* in Australia, Indonesia, the Philippines, Myanmar, and elsewhere in the tropical western Pacific. Colors range from white to gold.

Tahitian pearls

Pearls from the Black-lipped pearl oyster, *Pinctada margaritifera,* were discovered by Westerners in the waters off Tahiti and the neighboring Tuamoto Islands in 1827. In the late nineteenth and early twentieth centuries, over-fishing depleted these pearl reefs. Modern periculture began in Tahiti n 1965 and has grown rapidly: Pearls are once again French Polynesia's leading export. Colors range from gray to black.

Tsavorites

Green garnets from Kenya.

Unio pearls

Former term for freshwater pearls produced by the Unionidae family of mussels found in the rivers of North America, Scotland, Germany, France, Scandinavia, Russia, China, and elsewhere. About twenty-five North American species were fished for pearls in the nineteenth and early twentieth centuries.

Page numbers in *italics*
refer to illustrations.

PHOTOGRAPHY CREDITS

Unless noted otherwise in credits or in captions, all other drawings, objects, and photographs are © Tiffany & Co.

© Richard Avedon: 191

Eric Boman: 3, 179, 200, 275

Billy Cunningham: 20, 38–9, 52, 59, 80–81, 94–95, 133, 172, 183, 253, 256 (pages 20, 52, 59, 80–81, 94–95, 133, 172, 253, 256 are reprinted from *Tiffany Jewels,* published by Harry N. Abrams, Inc., 1999)

Condé Nast Publications, Inc.: 180 © 1939, 184 © 1933, 194 © 1970

Bill Diodato: 231

Gerald Foster: 270–71

François Halard: 218

Elizabeth Heyert: 11, 71, 157 (all are reprinted from *Tiffany's 150 Years,* published by Doubleday & Co., 1987)

Hiro: 292

Michael Jansson: 248–49

David Kelley: 49, 111, 255

Bill King, courtesy Janet McClelland: 239

Stan Malinowski: 214

Raymond Meier: 169

Sheila Metzner: 240

James Moore: 192

Paramount/Kobal: 173

Courtesy of Paramount Pictures and the Audrey Hepburn Children's Fund: front cover, 188–89. Photographs from *Breakfast at Tiffany's* © by Paramount Pictures. All rights reserved.

Linda Peckman: 265 (left), 268

Photographer unknown: 242

Ned Redway: 230

Matthew Rolston: 289

Jerry Salvati: 193

Kim Sargent: 122 (right)

Francesco Scavullo: 227

Skinner, Boston: 104

Victor Skrebneski: 215

Sølve Sundsbø: 288

Walter Thomson: 1

COLLECTION CREDITS

A La Vieille Russie: 94–95 (necklace)

Art Institute of Chicago: 122 (left), gift of an anonymous donor, Mr. and Mrs. James Alsdorf, Mrs. Lester Armour, and Mrs. George B. Young

The Bowes Museum, Barnard Castle, England: 29

Château de Compiègne, Réunion des Musées Nationaux/Art Resource, New York: 24

Chicago Historical Society: 40, 100–01

Christie's Images: 153

Collection the author: 124

Collection unknown: 19

Edimedia, Paris: 24, 72–73, 133 (background)

© Flagler Museum: 156

Historical Portraits Ltd: 25, by kind permission of Philip Mould

Friends of Iolani Palace, Honolulu: 23, gift of John Loring

Kunstgewerbemuseum, Berlin: 122 (right)

Kunsthistoriches Museum, Vienna: 16 (left)

Neil Lane, Los Angeles: 163

Fred Leighton Rare Collectable Jewels: 133 (necklace)

Musée Condé, Réunion des Musées Nationaux/Art Resource, New York: 14

Museum of the City of New York: 51, gift of Mrs. Edward C. Moen, 62.234.1A–C

National Portrait Gallery, London: 12, 13

New-York Historical Society: 32, 34 (bottom)

© Patrimonio Nacional, Monasterio de las Descalsa Reales, Madrid: 16 (right), 21

© Elsa Peretti: 292

Private collections: 20 (necklace), 182, 255

Private collection, Lafayette, California: 166

James Robinson, Inc., New York: 52

The Royal Collection © 2005, Her Majesty Queen Elizabeth II: 76

Smithsonian Institution, National Portrait Gallery: 37

Stiftung Preußische Schlösser und Gärten Berlin–Brandenburg, Potsdam: 22

Rare Book and Special Collections Division of the Library of Congress, Washington, DC: 36

Louis Comfort Tiffany Garden Museum, Matsue, Japan: 162, 164–65

V & A Images/Victoria and Albert Museum, London: 17

Walters Art Museum, Baltimore: 119

Wartski, London: 154

ACKNOWLEDGMENTS

The author and Tiffany & Co. would first like to thank Michael Kowalski, chairman and chief executive officer of Tiffany & Co., for his enthusiastic support during the evolution of *Tiffany Pearls*.

Special recognition is richly deserved by Eric Erickson, whose graphic contributions have brought out the best in the rich and complex imagery that present Tiffany pearls in all their splendor; Kay Olson Freeman, whose research brought to light so much of the rich textured history of pearls; and Rollins Maxwell, for his insightful captions and glossary that succinctly reveal a wealth of intriguing details about the many types of pearls and their adventures in the world of jewelry. This book is as much theirs as it is the author's.

We owe more thanks to MaryAnn Aurora who maintained calm and order and good will while trafficking the materials and personalities involved under an impossibly tight schedule; to Eric Himmel, editor-in-chief of Harry N. Abrams, Inc., for his friendship and unflagging support for all who contributed to this book's realization; to Andrea Danese, our pearl of an editor at Abrams who championed the cause throughout with vigor, charm, style, and imagination; to Russell Hassell, our so talented designer, for his genius at discovering all the visual echoes and stylish details in the history of *Tiffany Pearls* and for the pure visual excitement his ideas created; and to our copyeditor, Carrie Hornbeck, for the clarity she brought to the text.

Special recognition is due the photographers: the late Richard Avedon, Eric Boman, Adam Campanella, Sean Byrnes, Billy Cunningham, Bill Diodato, Gerald Foster, Martin Friedman, Phil Garfield, François Halard, Elizabeth Heyert, Hiro, David Kelly, the late Bill King, Stan Malinowski, Raymond Meier, Sheila Metzner, Thomas Milewski, James Moore, Linda Peckman, Ned Redway, Matthew Rolston, Jerry Salvati, the late Francesco Scavullo, Victor Skrebneski, Sølve Sundsbø, and Walter Thomson.

The author's eternal gratitude goes to the wonderful Sarah Jessica Parker for creating and lending her disarming image of a twenty-first century "Holly Golightly" to *Tiffany Pearls* forty-five years after her predecessor, Audrey Hepburn, had for *Breakfast at Tiffany's*.

We are also grateful to Annamarie Sandecki, Tiffany's director of Tiffany archives, for her help with the ongoing adventure of exploring Tiffany & Co.'s treasure trove of archival documents, drawings, and photographs; Louisa Bann, Tiffany's manager of research services, for her generous-spirited support and guidance in the bewildering complexities of our archives; Meghan Magee, registrar of the archives, for orchestrating the reproduction of archival materials; and Katherine Collins, archives associate.

And finally, considerable thanks to all who were invaluable in providing illustrations: Suzanne Aaron of Tiffany's marketing division; Linda Buckley, vice president of Tiffany's public relations media division; Christie's; Condé Nast; Alastair Duncan; John Blades, director of the Flagler Museum; *Harper's Bazaar*; Neil Lane; Fred Leighton; Pierce MacGuire of Tiffany's Schlumberger jewelry division; Janet McClelland's Bill King archive; Caroline Naggiar, Tiffany's senior vice president of marketing; Paramount Pictures; Primavera Gallery; James Robinson, NY; Stephen – Russell, NY; The Louis Comfort Tiffany Garden Museum; *Town & Country* magazine; Wartski, London; and the Audrey Hepburn Children's Fund.

Editor: Andrea Danese
Designer: Russell Hassell
Production Manager: Anet Sirna-Bruder

Library of Congress Cataloging-in-Publication Data

Loring, John.
   Tiffany pearls / by John Loring.
       p.   cm.
   Includes index.
   ISBN 0-8109-5443-5 (hardcover)
   1. Pearl jewelry—History. 2. Tiffany and Company. I. Title.

NK7680.L67 2006
739.27—dc22   2006010800

Printed and bound in Japan
10 9 8 7 6 5 4 3 2 1

harry n. abrams, inc.
a subsidiary of La Martinière Groupe

115 West 18th Street
New York, NY 10011
www.hnabooks.com

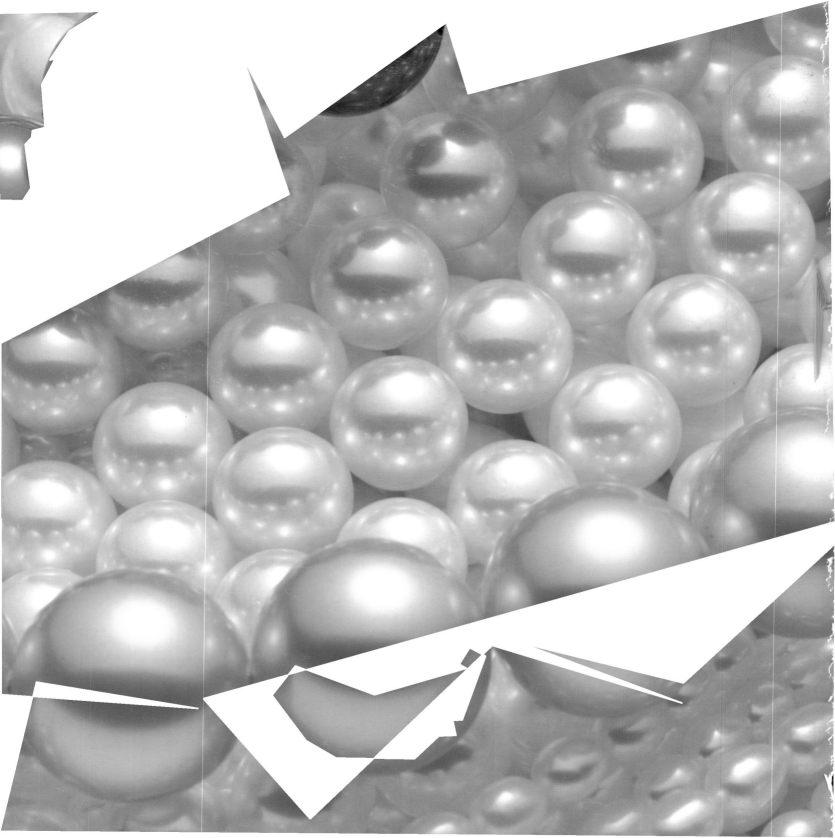